W9-AUB-846

# CLASSIC
## BOOKS

# Our Freedom to Read

● ● ● ● ● ● ● ● ● ● ●

**Coming-of-Age Fiction**

**Outsider Fiction**

**Classic Books**

**Science Fiction and Fantasy**

# CLASSIC
## BOOKS

STEVEN OTFINOSKI

**CHELSEA HOUSE PUBLISHERS**

An imprint of Infobase Publishing

# CLASSIC BOOKS

Chelsea House
An imprint of Infobase Publishing
132 West 31st Street
New York NY 10001

**Library of Congress Cataloging-in-Publication Data**
Otfinoski, Steven.
Our freedom to read / Steven Otfinoski.
v. cm.
Includes bibliographical references and indexes.
Contents: [1] Classic books—[2] Coming-of-age fiction—
[3] Outsider fiction—[4] Science fiction and fantasy.
ISBN 978-1-60413-029-4 (v. 1 : acid-free paper)—ISBN 978-1-60413-030-0 (v. 2 : acid-free
paper)—ISBN 978-1-60413-031-7 (v. 3 : acid-free paper)—ISBN 978-1-60413-032-4 (v. 4 :
acid-free paper) 1. Prohibited books—Bibliography—Juvenile literature. 2. Challenged
books—Bibliography—Juvenile literature. 3. Expurgated books—Bibliography—Juvenile
literature. 4. Prohibited books—United States—Bibliography—Juvenile literature. 5. Challenged books—United States—Bibliography—Juvenile literature. 6. Expurgated books—
United States—Bibliography—Juvenile literature. 7. Children's stories—Censorship—United
States—Case studies—Juvenile literature. 8. Young adult fiction—Censorship—United
States—Case studies—Juvenile literature. 9. Children's stories—Bio-bibliography—Juvenile
literature. 10. Young adult fiction—Bio-bibliography—Juvenile literature. I. Title.
Z1019.O84 2009        098'.1—dc22
2008032030

Text design by Erika K. Arroyo
Cover design by Ben Peterson

Printed in the United States of America

Bang FOF 10 9 8 7 6 5 4 3 2 1

This book is printed on acid-free paper.

# Contents

# Introduction

JAMES JOYCE, ONE OF THE GREAT WRITERS OF THE TWENTIETH century, was told by his publisher that he had to take out the "offensive words" in his short-story collection *Dubliners* or it wouldn't be printed.

"I can't alter what I have written," Joyce replied. "[If I had listened to] all the objections I would not have written the book . . . I can't write without offending people."

Joyce's uncompromising stance on his work is common among many of the great writers of classic literature. It may be one of the reasons why their work has stood the test of time. They wrote from their deepest feelings and convictions, not to please the world they lived in. They wrote for the ages, not for the current fashion of society.

Joyce went on to write *Ulysses*, a book many critics believe is the greatest novel of the twentieth century. *Ulysses* took its inspiration from another classic: the ancient Greek epic *The Odyssey*. Few modern works have had as long and torturous a censorship history as *Ulysses*.

The 13 classic books in this volume are a varied lot and share only two things in common—they are truly "classics" that have passed the test of time, and they have all been read and enjoyed by young readers, from grade school to secondary school. Some, like *Little Black Sambo*, were written specifically for children. Others, such as *Gulliver's Travels*, *The Adventures of Huckleberry Finn*, and *Animal Farm*, have imaginative premises that appeal to children, but under the surface are anything but childlike in their sharp criticism of society.

The Bible and *The Arabian Nights*, two literary works not normally linked together, are many books in one and vast treasure houses of stories. Many of their tales appeal to young people, but others deal with sexuality and violence that are intended for adults.

The social realism of *Oliver Twist,* the *Little House* books, *Of Mice and Men,* and *Black Boy* have made them favorites with young readers and, for the last two, staples of high school reading lists. But that same realism in language and action has made them controversial, especially in their reflection of times when African Americans, Jews, and Native Americans were the victims of social prejudice and racism.

The coming-of-age sagas of Holden Caulfield in *The Catcher in the Rye* and Scout in *To Kill a Mockingbird* are modern-day classics. But the unique viewpoints of the young protagonists and that of the adult world that surrounds them have made them favorite targets of classroom and school library challengers.

Being "classics" has not protected any of these books from the attacks of angry parents, righteous school boards, responsive superintendents, and the general public. From the Bible to *To Kill a Mockingbird,* these books have been misunderstood, misread, and abused. Yet their power has not been diminished or their popularity dimmed by all the challenges and censorship.

While there are many more contemporary fiction and nonfiction books that have drawn the fire of challengers, many of these classic books remain targets of censorship. *The Catcher in the Rye,* for example, published in 1951, was ranked number three by the American Library Association (ALA) on its list of "10 Most Frequently Challenged Books of 2005." *The Adventures of Huckleberry Finn* (1885) and *Of Mice and Men* (1937) were ranked fifth and sixth, respectively, on the ALA's list of "100 Most Frequently Challenged Books of 1990–2000."

## Challenges, Censorship, and This Book

What exactly is a challenge to a book? The ALA, founded in 1876, monitors challenges and defines a book challenge as a "formal, written complaint filed with a library or school requesting that materials be removed because of content or appropriateness." According to the ALA, there were 546 book challenges in 2006, an increase of 30 percent from 2005. The organization considers that number in "the midrange," and rather low compared to the peak years of the mid-1990s, when book challenges numbered more than 750 annually. Some experts attribute the surge at that time to the appearance of the *Harry Potter* series, one of the most challenged book series of all time.

Why does the ALA care about these challenges and monitor them so closely? "One of the things we believe is that materials need to be available to people so that they can make their own choices," former Associate Director of the ALA's Office for Intellectual Freedom Cynthia Robinson has said. "Removing books suppresses that point of view . . . The First Amendment is very important to librarians and one of our most important rights as Americans. It's so fundamental I think people often take it for granted . . . supporting intellectual freedom [and] the right of individuals and their families to decide what they're going to read is one of the association's most important missions and by far one of its most public."

Most book challenges noted by the ALA are made initially by parents of students who become aware of a book's content when their child brings it home to read or study. In many cases these challengers reject the honest depiction of the real world—and the language and behavior of those who inhabit it. Some adults do not care for their children to know what life is like in the netherworld of the drug addict or behind the locked gates of a boys' reformatory or a psychiatric hospital. Other challenges arise over the very issues that the authors are challenging and criticizing, such as physical or sexual child abuse, racism, and bullying in schools. Still others resent the proposition put forth in a number of these books that it is largely the system—whether school administrators, misguided parents, or corrupt governments—that is to blame for the injustices depicted. They are disturbed by the authors' sharp criticism of authority in all its forms.

When a formal challenge is made, the school district takes it seriously. In most cases, the school board or school superintendent will turn the matter over to a special review committee for consideration. The committee may already be established, or in many cases may only be formed when needed. The committee members may include school administrators, media specialists, teachers, parents, area residents, and even students. The challenged book may continue to remain in use in the school or in circulation in the school library while the committee is deliberating, although in some cases the book is removed during this period.

After reading the challenged book, possibly hearing more from the challengers, and discussing the matter among themselves, the committee members come up with a recommendation that is passed on to the school board. The school board then meets to consider the recommendation and votes to either accept the recommendation as it is or make another decision about the challenged book. Sometimes the school superintendent will play an important role in this process.

Many challenges are rejected. According to Judith Krug, director of the ALA's Office for Intellectual Freedom, only 30 out of the 546 challenged books were actually banned in 2006. These bans can take several forms. Some result in the complete removal of a book from the classroom and school library. In other cases, the book is taken from the classroom but is retained on the school library shelves, sometimes with limited access for certain grades or to be borrowed only with written parental permission. In still other cases, the challenged book is removed from one grade but taught in a higher grade where it is considered more appropriate.

Some book challenges are questionable or even absurd. In one case, parents in McKinleyville, California, challenged the joke book *Laugh Lines* in 1990 and wanted it removed from the elementary school library. The challenge claimed it was "demeaning" toward readers who read the riddles and couldn't come up with the correct answers. Other challenges are trivial. One parent, noted in a "Landmark Challenge" in this series, complained about the single use of a swear word by a character in a novel. Some challenges are misguided. According to the ALA, the most challenged book in both 2006 and 2007 was the children's picture book *And Tango Makes Three,* the true story of two male penguins that raise a baby penguin without a female. Parents complained that the book promoted a homosexual lifestyle. The same book was praised by the ALA as one of the best picture books of 2006.

"So many adults are exhausting themselves worrying about other people corrupting their children with books, they're turning kids off to reading instead of turning them on," wrote Judy Blume in the introduction to a collection of stories by banned writers. "In this age of censorship I mourn the loss of books that will never be written, I mourn the voices that will be silenced—writers' voices, teachers' voices, students' voices—and all because of fear."

The most important part of this volume is not the description of the challenges themselves but that of the courageous voices that rose up in opposition, to support these books and to defend them. In many cases they made the difference—ending a challenge or bringing a banned book back into the classroom or back on to the library shelf. These books are a cry for tolerance and justice in our world. They stand up for diversity and the differences that make us each unique individuals. If we deny ourselves their wisdom, wit, and power, we will all end up as the ultimate losers—estranged from one another, society, and ourselves.

The format of this book is straightforward. Each entry covers a single banned or challenged book or series of books, presented in chronological order by date of publication. Entries start with a concise summary of the book in the "What Happens in" section. This is followed by "Challenges and Censorship," which may include some or all of the following: the history of how the author came to write the book, its initial reception from reviewers and readers, and the main reasons why it has been challenged in schools. Next is one or more "Landmark Challenges" described in detail. Some landmark challenges include several related challenges. Finally, each entry concludes with a list of sources for "Further Reading" and a brief biography of the author or authors in "About the Author of."

Why a series about book banning? Can we learn something from these cases of challenges and censorship of classic fiction? The American Library Association thinks so, which is why it reports on challenges from around the nation and the world in its monthly *Newsletter on Intellectual Freedom,* a publication now more than a half century old. The ALA also sponsors Banned Books Week each year to focus attention on books that have been banned.

"Throughout history, there always have been a few people who don't want information to be freely available. And this is still true," said ALA President Leslie Burger during Banned Books Week 2006. "The reason more books aren't banned is because community residents—with librarians, teachers, and journalists—stand up and speak out for their freedom to read." As long as we all recognize censorship when it arises and speak out against it, that freedom will remain secure.

# *The Bible*

## What Happens in the Bible

The Bible is the holy book of both the Jewish and Christian religions. It is actually a collection of numerous separate books and includes a variety of literary forms—historical narrative, stories, poems, prayers, letters, and proverbs. In the Roman Catholic and Protestant bibles these books are divided into two distinct sections, named the Old Testament and the New Testament. The Jewish, or Hebrew, Bible omits the New Testament.

The first five books of the Hebrew Bible, often called the Pentateuch, depict man's fall from grace to sin; the founding of the Jewish religion in the Middle East by Abraham and his descendants; the enslavement of the Israelites, the Jewish people, by the Egyptians; and their escape from Egypt under the leadership of Moses. Later books describe the Israelites' settlement in the land of Palestine, the Holy Land; the establishment of a kingdom under a series of kings; its division into two kingdoms; the eventual downfall of both kingdoms during an invasion by the Babylonians; and the Israelites' eventual return to their holy city of Jerusalem.

The New Testament depicts events from the birth of Jesus, a Jew who founded Christianity, to about 100 C.E. (Common Era). It tells about the life, teachings, and death of Jesus, whom Christians believe is the son of God, and the development of the early Christian church under the leadership of the apostles, especially Peter and Paul. The New Testament includes 21 books of letters or epistles, written to members of early Christian communities by church leaders, and the

13

Book of Revelation, which tells about events leading up to the Last Judgment on earth and the return of Jesus Christ.

## Challenges and Censorship

Many of the individuals who have challenged books in classrooms and school libraries have been deeply religious people who derive their values and mores from the Bible. But the Bible itself, in its two-millennium history, has been challenged, banned, censored, and burned for a host of reasons. These acts of censorship have been rooted in keeping the Bible from being translated into modern languages, removing passages of sinful and unmoral behavior of people in the Bible, and removing the Bible from American public schools as an issue of church vs. state.

## Landmark Challenge: Holy War Against Translations

The original Old Testament was written in Hebrew and the New Testament in Greek. Both were later translated into Latin by St. Jerome and others. Since early times authorities of both church and state were strictly opposed to translating God's word into other languages, for several reasons. First, if translated into another tongue, the Bible might be misinterpreted or misunderstood. Second, people feared that a translator could put his or her own spin on God's word and use it for distorted ends, as some believed the Protestants did when they translated the Bible into German and other languages. Finally, many upper-class people believed that it was dangerous to make the Bible available in the national language of the common folk, especially women and poor working people. They believed that these "benighted" persons had neither the judgment nor intelligence to read the Bible and understand it for themselves. They needed to have the Bible interpreted for them by church officials and others.

For all these reasons, translations of the Bible were forbidden for more than 1,300 years. One of the first leaders to ban Bible translations was the Roman Emperor Justinian, who issued a decree in 553 allowing use of only the Greek and Latin versions. During the Middle Ages, Latin largely remained the official language of both church and state, and there were few attempts to translate the Bible.

But soon, courageous individuals emerged who sought to make the Bible available to the masses of people in their homelands. One of the most important of these was John Wycliffe, who translated the Bible into English in the late fourteenth century. Wycliffe believed that all people had the right to read the Gospel "in that tongue in which they knew best Christ's teaching."

In 1409 the Synod, or meeting, of Canterbury convened at St. Paul's Cathedral in London and issued a decree stating that all translations of the Bible were forbidden and that anyone reading a new translation without a special license would be excommunicated, or cut off, from the Roman Catholic Church.

When Martin Luther and other clergymen broke with the Catholic Church during the Protestant Reformation, they declared that the individual should have the right to read and interpret the Bible for him or herself. The Englishman William Tyndale refused to give in to the Church and translated the Old Testament. Knowing his work and life were in danger in England, Tyndale fled to Cologne, Germany, where his English Bible was published in 1525 and 1526. Six thousand sheets of Tyndale's Bible were then smuggled into England—and became the first book to be officially banned there. Confiscated copies were publicly burned at St. Paul's Cathedral, and Tyndale was arrested in Antwerp, Belgium, and imprisoned. He was condemned for heresy and in October 1536 was strangled and his body burned along with copies of his Bible.

In 1546 the Roman Catholic Council of Trent met and decreed that the Latin Vulgate Bible translated by St. Jerome was the only true authorized text. It remained so until the end of the eighteenth century. Ironically, when an English version of the Bible was finally commissioned and written in 1611, it relied heavily on Tyndale's Bible. Some scholars claim nine-tenths of the King James Version (KJV) is taken directly from Tyndale's Bible, although he was not given credit.

## Landmark Challenge: "Cleaning Up" the Bible

By the late eighteenth century the focus of those censoring the Bible shifted from the issue of translation to its actual content. Many godfearing reformers came to the conclusion that parts of the Bible—

namely passages that dealt with violence and sex—were not fit for "good" Christians to read.

One of the first attempts in English to expurgate the Bible (which means to alter it by removing objectionable material) is credited to Dr. Edward Harwood and his *Liberal Translation of the New Testament,* which appeared in 1768. Harwood's goal was to transform "the bald and barbarous language of the old vulgar version with up-to-date elegance." Here is an example of Harwood's elegant English rewrite of the beginning of the Lord's Prayer:

> O Thou great governour and parent of universal nature—who manifestest thy glory to the blessed inhabitants of heaven—may all thy rational creatures in all the parts of thy boundless dominion be happy in the knowledge of thy existence and providence . . . .

Like many an expurgator after him, Harwood focused his efforts on young readers, hoping that "YOUTH could be allured by the innocent stratagems of a *modern style,* to read a book which is now, alas! Too generally neglected by the young and gay."

Another man with a mission was John Bellamy, who proudly called his 1818 work *The Holy Bible, Newly Translated by John Bellamy.* Bellamy came to the original assumption that the great men and women of the Bible could not be capable of wrongdoing and that if the Bible said they were sinners, it could only be the fault of the original translators from the Hebrew. To correct this situation, Bellamy spent 10 years learning Hebrew in order to do his own translation. Sometimes Bellamy's improvements were little more than rationalizations. For instance, in Genesis 9 Noah gets drunk in his tent. In Bellamy's version, Noah "is satisfied with the wine," not drunk from it. Some of England's most distinguished people, including several members of the royal family, lined up to subscribe to the work. But biblical scholars found his efforts a sham. "[H]e is . . . truly destitute of judgment," said theologian George D'Oyly. In time, Bellamy's wealthy patrons deserted him. He continued his work until his money ran out, and then was forced to abandon it.

In 1824 Church of England layperson John Watson came out with his *Holy Bible Arranged and Adapted for Family Reading.* Watson's eccentric editing of the Bible removed the traditional chapters and verses and replaced them with his own sectional divisions. Some objectionable books such as the Song of Solomon, which compares earthly, physical love to divine love, were completely omitted in defense of good taste. A note under the title explained it was better not to expose young readers to this book "lest in the fervor of youth they give too wide a scope to fancy, and interpret to a bad sense the spirited ideas of Solomon."

Quaker printer William Alexander took Watson's idea a step further in his 1828 *Holy Book Principally Designed to Facilitate the Audible or Social Reading of the Sacred Scriptures*. Alexander's eccentric design separated the Bible's books into general topics with names like Devotional Section, General Section, and a Personal Perusal Section, in which he dumped all objectionable passages. He freely eliminated any detail or passage "not congenial to the views and genius of the present age of refinement." The chaotic format, however, put off readers, making Alexander's Bible an utter failure.

## Landmark Challenge: Noah Webster Tackles the Bible

The history of biblical censorship in the United States began in the colonial period. The British crown retained the copyright of the English Bible and forbade it to be printed in the American colonies. However, a Bible was printed secretly in Philadelphia in 1782. After American independence, bibles were routinely printed, mostly the King James Version.

No less a literary light than Noah Webster, author of the first successful American dictionary, decided that the King James Version, in name alone, was not a proper Bible for the new republic. Webster called his Bible, which he began work on in 1821, "the most important enterprise of my life." It was the language of the KJV that most bothered Webster, and he set out to produce a Bible "free of words offensive to modesty . . . by correcting a few obvious errors, and removing some obscurities, with objectionable words and phrases . . . . "

Webster, who lived in Connecticut, sent samples of his work to the Andover Theological Seminary in Massachusetts. Biblical scholars there were not impressed. Webster returned to work on his *American Dictionary of the English Language*, which was published in 1828, and then resumed work on his Bible in 1830. While he left intact every incident in the Bible, Webster changed the words in thousands of passages, especially in the Old Testament. In Webster's expurgated Bible, objects and people didn't stink but rather gave off "an odious scent." People and animals didn't have "buttocks" but "hind-parts," and a man didn't "lust" after a woman but only "desired" her.

Webster's Bible was published in New Haven, Connecticut, in 1835. It was officially adopted by the State of Connecticut and even endorsed by Yale University, his alma mater. But few readers preferred its delicate language to the earthy and more vivid King James Version. The Webster Bible disappeared by the early 1840s after only two printings.

# Landmark Challenge:
# Abington Township School District v. Schempp

In modern America, challenges to the Bible, especially in schools and school libraries, have been based not on translation or language issues as much as on the ongoing debate of church vs. state. That burning question has focused on whether the Bible should be used for religious purposes in public schools or only as a literary text studied as history or literature.

In 1962 Edward Schempp, a resident of Abington Township, Pennsylvania, and a member of the Unitarian church, filed a suit against the local school district in federal district court. Schempp's suit protested a state law that required his son Ellery and all other public school children to listen to and sometimes read verses from the Bible each morning in class. The law required that "[a]t least ten verses from the Holy Bible [be] read, without comment, at the opening of each public school on each school day." Schempp claimed that the law violated his son's and other family members' rights under the First Amendment to the U.S. Constitution, which allows for freedom of religion, and the Fourteenth Amendment, which identifies the civil rights of all Americans.

When the case came to trial, Schempp testified that the daily Biblical readings expressed religious beliefs "which were contrary to the religious beliefs which they held and to their familial teaching." The district court ruled in Schempp's favor and removed the state law from the books. The school district appealed the ruling and, in the interim, state legislators amended the law, allowing students to be excused from the religious exercises with the written permission of their parents. Schempp found this unacceptable and went forward with another suit. Again, the district court ruled in his favor. In its decision the court said, "The reading of the verses, even without comment, possesses a devotional and religious character and constitutes in effect a religious observance."

The school district appealed twice to the U.S. Supreme Court to take the case. It finally agreed to do so and heard the case on February 27 and 28, 1963. Four months later it gave its ruling. The vote was 7 to 1 in Edward Schempp's favor. In a 73-page opinion, Justice William J. Brennan spelled out the Court's intentions. "Whatever [presidents] Jefferson or Madison would have thought of Bible reading or the recital of the Lord's Prayer in . . . public schools . . . our use of the history . . . must limit itself to broad purposes, not specific practices," he wrote. Matters of religion belonged in the church and religious schools, not the public school system, which had to adhere to a strict separation of church and state, as laid down in the Constitution.

Justice Potter Stewart, who cast the lone dissenting vote, disagreed: "If religious exercises are held to be an impermissible activity in schools, religion is placed in an artificial and state-created disadvantage . . . And a refusal to permit religious exercises thus is seen, not as the realization of state neutrality, but rather as the establishment of a religion of secularism . . . . "

Public opinion on this landmark decision was sharply divided. Evangelical Protestants opposed it, while mainline Protestants, such as Methodists and Lutherans, applauded it. Many Catholics were against it, while Jews supported it. "God and religion have all but been driven from the public schools," said the *Washington Evening Star*. "Will . . . Christmas carols be the next to go?"

The issue of school prayer and Bible reading continues to be a hot topic for many members of the religious right. Conservatives have even worked to add an amendment to the Constitution to allow for these activities in schools and public places.

## Landmark Challenge: Turning the Tables

Atheist Gene Kasmar called on the Brooklyn Center school district in Minnesota to remove the Bible from schools in July 1992. "The lewd, indecent, and violent contents of that book are hardly suitable for young students," wrote Kasmar. "The Bible quickly reveals its unsuitability in a school and learning environment."

Kasmar's supporters in the Minnesota Atheists group endorsed his challenge in an article in the *Minneapolis Star-Tribune*. "Neither Kasmar nor Minnesota Atheists endorses censorship," the group made clear. "We support the constitutional guarantees of free speech and reject any action that stifles education and communication . . . We commend Kasmar for turning the tables on the religious right, which has long been engaged in a relentless campaign to censor materials it dislikes. By using the religious right's own criteria for what is unsuitable for impressionable children to read—lewd language, explicit sex, incest, satanism, drunkenness, violence, and witchcraft—Kasmar shows the Bible to be censorable. What goes around comes around."

In November the District 286 Board of Education decided by unanimous vote to keep the Bible in the district's two school libraries. Kasmar called the decision "a sad commentary on the intrusion of religion into our public school system." In a pamphlet he wrote and distributed, Kasmar issued this warning to the educators: "If you don't want the Bible censored, don't try to censor other books. People who set the rules and criteria for removing books probably ought to look to their own house."

In Fairbanks, Alaska, James Petersen tried a similar challenge against the Bible in March 1993, albeit with a somewhat different motive. "My intentions were not to hurt, to insult, or to degrade anyone's faith. Or to scare the tar out of people," Petersen said. He was merely reacting to the Noel Wien Library's removal of a favorite graphic novel to the reserve desk because it was deemed too violent and pornographic. "I felt something had to be stated about what happens when you start banning books," he said. His complaint that the Bible should be banned because it was "obscene and pornographic" was rejected unanimously by the library commission at a public meeting on March 17.

"I knew darned well that the library commission would say no," Petersen said after the meeting. However, he held to his point that if the Bible had been made into a comic book, like the work put on reserve, "there would be many objecting to it."

American author Mark Twain, whose *Huckleberry Finn* is one of the most challenged books in the United States, had a similar thought back in 1907 when he wrote, "The truth is, that when a Library expels a book of mine and leaves an unexpurgated Bible around where unprotected youth and age can get hold of it, the deep unconscious irony of it delights me and doesn't anger me."

After 2,000 years of controversy, the Bible remains the best-selling book of all time and will likely remain so.

## Further Reading

"Brooklyn Center, Minnesota." *Newsletter on Intellectual Freedom,* January 1993: 8–9; March 1993: 55–56.

"Fairbanks, Alaska." *Newsletter on Intellectual Freedom,* July 1993: 123.

Foerstel, Herbert N. *Banned in the U.S.A.: A Reference Guide to Book Censorship in Schools and Public Libraries.* Westport, Conn.: Greenwood Press, 2002.

Haight, Anne Lyon, and Chandler B. Grannis. *Banned Books: 387 B.C. to 1978 A.D.* New York: R. R. Bowker, 1978.

Karolides, Nicholas J., Margaret Bald, and Dawn B. Sova. *120 Banned Books: Censorship Histories of World Literature.* New York: Facts On File, 2005.

Perrin, Noel. *Dr. Bowdler's Legacy: A History of Expurgated Books in England and America.* New York: Atheneum, 1969.

## About the Authors of the Bible

Just as the Bible is made up of many books, it has many authors, most of them unknown. The adherents of Judaism and Christianity attribute certain books of the Old and New testaments to certain biblical figures, although there is little hard evidence that these people actually wrote the books themselves. For instance, in the Old Testament, tradition says that Moses wrote the Pentateuch, King David wrote the Book of Psalms, and the prophet Isaiah wrote the two books named after him. Most of the Old Testament was handed down orally over hundreds of years, however, and then written down and edited by many writers. An assembly of Jewish rabbis established the authorized text, or canon, around 100 C.E., and a standard text of the book was completed around 150.

The New Testament also has many authors, although the four gospels, or lives of Jesus, may have been written by the four apostles they are named after—Mark, Matthew, Luke, and John. Luke is also traditionally named the author of the Acts of the Apostles, a narrative of the early church. Of the 21 letters or epistles to members of early Christian communities, the first 13 are attributed to St. Paul, the church's first important missionary. The last 8 letters were probably written by other church leaders imitating the style and content of Paul's letters. All of the letters were written, biblical scholars believe, between the 50s and about 125 C.E. The last book of the New Testament, Revelation, was written by a man named John, who probably was not the same John who wrote the Gospel. By 400 C.E. the books of the New Testament were authorized as a canon and written down as a text.

# The Arabian Nights
## (c. 800–900)
### by Anonymous
### (translated by Richard Burton)

• • • • • • • • • • • • •

## What Happens in *The Arabian Nights*

This collection of Eastern folk tales, also known as *One Thousand and One Nights,* is framed in an intriguing tale of its own. In early times, Sultan Shahryar, or Schahriah, of Persia discovers that his wife and her lover have plotted to kill him. He has them both executed and comes to believe that all women are unfaithful by nature. For three years, he marries a new wife each night and at daybreak has her strangled. The country becomes distraught at the loss of so many young, marriageable women. Scheherazade, the clever daughter of the vizier, the sultan's chief adviser, comes up with a plan to end the carnage. She volunteers to become the sultan's next wife but insists that her sister Dinarzade live with her in the palace. On her wedding night, an hour before daybreak, Scheherazade begins to tell Dinarzade a story. The sultan listens in and becomes engrossed in the tale. At dawn, Scheherazade abruptly stops the story, leaving it unfinished. Shahryar, desperate to hear how the story ends, agrees to let her live another day. That night, she continues the tale but leaves it again unfinished. This continues, story by story, for a thousand and one nights. During this time Scheherazade and the sultan have three sons and she proves her faithfulness to him. At the end of the last night, Shahryar pardons his wife and, as in all fairy tales, they live happily ever after.

The stories that Scheherazade tells are of many different styles, including adventure stories, comic stories, and romantic stories. Several of them have become children's classics. "Sinbad the Sailor" is the tale of a Baghdad merchant who goes on seven adventurous voyages, where he encounters a one-eyed giant called the Cyclops, a legendary bird called the Roc, and the Old Man of the Sea. "Ali Baba and the 40 Thieves" tells of a poor woodcutter who outwits a band of robbers who keep their booty in a secret cave that will open at the magic words "Open, sesame." "Aladdin's Lamp" is about a poor boy who discovers a magical lamp in a cave. When he rubs the lamp, two genies appear to fulfill his every wish.

Many of the other tales are more adult in nature, especially in the 1885–86 translation of Sir Richard Burton, who was more faithful to the original stories than most other translators. Although Scheherazade's stories lasted for a thousand and one nights, the complete collection includes only 270 tales; they originated from India, Persia (today Iran), Iraq, Turkey, and possibly Greece.

## Challenges and Censorship

Interestingly, the original Arabic version of *The Arabian Nights* itself was never highly regarded in Eastern culture. "I have seen the complete work more than once," wrote Ali Aboulhusor el Mesoudi, a famous tenth-century historian, "and it is indeed a vulgar, insipid book." Folk tales were looked down on as one of the lowest forms of literary endeavor in medieval Arabic culture, inferior to such highly stylized literary forms as the *maqama*, a form of rhymed prose.

But the work achieved lasting popularity with Western audiences once it was translated, and generations of American and British children have marveled at the adventures of Sinbad the Sailor, Ali Baba, and Aladdin. Few know that many of the stories in *The Arabian Nights* contain explicit sexual passages, since most translators have removed the sexual content from these stories or completely omitted the stories that contain sexual references.

However, the most famous translation, made by Sir Richard Burton in 1885 in 10 volumes, with 6 volumes added later, included all the earthiness of the original. This has led to the work's censorship for more than a century.

## Landmark Challenge: Burton's Racy Translation

Sir Richard Burton had dealt with censorship of his work long before he wrote his translation, entitled *The Book of the Thousand Nights and a Night*. In 1856 the publisher of his travel book *First Footsteps in East Africa* tore out its appendix. The appendix, written in Latin, dealt with sexual customs of certain East African tribes that Burton had traveled among.

In 1883, to avoid such censorship, Burton and his partner translator, Eastern literature expert Forster Fitzgerald Arbuthnot, founded their own private publishing "house," the Kama Shastra Society, with fictitious headquarters in Benares, India. Burton's first published work under this banner was his translation of *The Kama Sutra of Vatsyayana* (1883), the classic Hindu marriage manual written about 300 B.C.E. (Before the Common Era). Realizing the sexual content of *The Kama Sutra* would bring the wrath of the censors down on him, Burton sold the book privately by subscription for the princely sum of about $200 in today's currency, and had "For Private Circulation Only" printed on the cover. When rogue American publisher Samuel Roth produced an edition of the book in the United States, he was targeted by the New York Society for the Suppression of Vice, arrested, and sentenced to 90 days in jail. Roth had earlier published an unauthorized version of James Joyce's controversial novel *Ulysses,* which also landed him in jail.

Burton followed the same publishing pattern with *The Arabian Nights.* Only a thousand copies were printed and sold to subscribers, again at about $200. Burton pretended his work was intended exclusively for an audience of Victorian gentlemen and male scholars who shared his fascination with Eastern literature, culture, and sexual practices. But the general public bought up most copies. The entire printing sold out, earning Burton the first income he had gained as an author—about $25,000.

While the reading public devoured the stories with the greatest of pleasure, the literary and social establishment of Victorian England was scandalized. One critic called the work "an extraordinary agglomerate of filth." Henry Reeve, a personal enemy of Burton, wrote a scathing review in the *Edinburgh Review,* one of the most influential periodicals in nineteenth-century Britain. According to Reeve, "probably no European has ever gathered such an appalling collection of degrading customs and statistics of vice. It is a work which no decent gentleman will long permit to stand upon his shelves." Then, comparing Burton with three other translators of *The Arabian Nights,* he concluded that "Galland is for the nursery, Lane for the library, Payne for the study, and Burton for the sewers."

Arabist Stanley Lane-Poole, whose uncle William Lane's translation was condemned by Burton, accused him of "an attitude of attraction towards all that is most repulsive in life and literature . . . the anthropological notes . . . evince an intimate acquaintance with Oriental depravity, the confession of which has at best the merit of boldness, whilst the elaborate exposition of so much filth can scarcely be a matter of congratulation." Other critics branded the book "absolutely unfit for the Christian population of the nineteenth century" and "offensive and not only offensive, but grossly and needlessly offensive."

There were those, however, who defended Burton's work and saw his faithful but imaginative translation as praiseworthy. "When we invite our youth to read an unexpurgated Bible, an unexpurgated collection of Elizabethan dramatists, including Shakespear," wrote poet and literary historian John Addington Symonds, "it is surely inconsistent to exclude the unexpurgated Arabian Nights, from the studies of a nation who rule India and administer Egypt." ("To expurgate" is to remove objectionable material from a literary work.)

But it wasn't only the sexual content of Burton's book that bothered critics. They were also put off by his ornate use of archaic language meant to recreate the original early Arabic. Another piece in the *Edinburgh Review* declared, "Captain Burton's English is an unreadable compound of archaeology and slang, abounding in Americanisms, and full of an affected reaching after obsolete or foreign words and phrases." A reviewer in the *Nation* in 1890, the year that Burton died, described the style as "unreadable for its own sake" and the archaisms as "barbarisms." The entire work was nothing more than "a flat failure."

Burton's wife, Lady Isabel Burton, had helped him prepare his work and promote it, but she believed the sexual passages were not fit for female readers. To correct this, Lady Burton prepared an edited version suitable for mothers and daughters in what she described as "six pretty volumes." Only 457 copies of this expurgated edition sold in two years. "The public would have none it," Burton wrote happily in the notes to the *Supplemental Nights*, the six additional volumes he later published.

The Kama Shastra Society produced a third Burton work in 1886 —*The Perfumed Garden*, another sex manual, attributed to fifteenth-century author Sheikh Nefzaoui, which Burton called "a manual of erotology." Although sold privately, pirated copies of the book appeared on the European continent and in the English Midlands. Burton was busy completing a revised edition of this work, *The Scented Garden,* when he died in 1890. Within two weeks of his death, his wife, who abhorred her husband's fascination with Eastern sexual practices, destroyed the original manuscript of *The Scented Garden* and all his notes for it, along with the original manuscript of *The Arabian Nights.* The intellectual British community condemned her actions as monstrous.

Before her death in 1896, Lady Burton named William Coote, secretary of the National Vigilance Association, as her husband's literary executor. Coote's role might be better described as literary "executioner." He picked up where Lady Isabel left off and burned many of Burton's private papers, including his translation of *The Perfumed Garden* with his notes and revisions, which he had labored over for 14 years. Isabel's surviving sister burned still more of poor Burton's papers.

## Landmark Challenge:
## Anthony Comstock Meets His Match

In the United States, expurgated versions of Burton's classic were allowed, but the original book was banned from entering the country by the U.S. Customs Office. This led to a celebrated case in 1894 that involved no less a champion of censorship than the nineteenth-century reformer Anthony Comstock.

Comstock and the New York Society for the Suppression of Vice, for which he served as secretary, had been campaigning against the Worthington Book Company and its expensive editions of "obscene" literary classics since 1877, when it took action against its sale of French author Honoré de Balzac's *Droll Stories.* In 1885 Comstock again took action, this time to stop Worthington from selling lavish editions of *The Arabian Nights* and other literary classics, such as Henry Fielding's bawdy comic novel *Tom Jones* and Giovanni Boccaccio's *Decameron,* an Italian collection of equally racy stories. In one discreet advertisement for the set of books, Worthington pointed out that they were "not for women or children, nor the drawing room table or dentist's waiting room."

To the crusading Comstock the books were not fit for anyone, and his effort to prohibit their sale was one factor that led Worthington to declare bankruptcy nine years later. The company decided to sell off its classic editions to Joseph J. Little, a receiver in the United States. Comstock rose once again to the occasion. He opposed the sale and sued the book company for trying to sell works that were "unfit for general circulation."

According to an article in the *New York Times* in May 1894, Little had sent copies of some of the volumes to Comstock, perhaps to convince him they were more than smut, but to no avail. In a response to Little's second letter of appeal, an exasperated Comstock replied: "It is utterly impossible for me to find time to examine these books. I have had them now for two weeks and more, and some for much longer, and I am completely nauseated with that kind of rot."

When the case came to trial that same month, the judge, Morgan J. O'Brien, surprisingly ruled in favor of the book company. O'Brien's ruling had more to do with the format of the books than their content. In his opinion the buyers of these pricey editions were too rich and sophisticated to purchase them for the supposedly pornographic passages rather than the books' "literary merit" and perhaps "their worth as specimens of fine bookmaking." Judge O'Brien displayed a clear prejudice against the middle and lower classes of society when he noted that these expensive editions "would not be bought nor appreciated by the class of people from whom unclean publications ought to be withheld. They [the books] are not corrupting in their influence upon the young, for they are not likely to reach them."

The judge showed a greater understanding of literature and censorship when he declared that "a seeker after the sensual and degrading parts of a narrative may find in all these works, as in those of other great authors, something to satisfy his pruriency," but to condemn books for a few episodes "would compel the exclusion from circulation of a very large proportion of the works of fiction of the most famous writers of the English language."

While the judgment was a blow to censorship in the United States, it did little to dampen Anthony Comstock's ardor. By the time of his death in 1915, his nationwide crusade against "indecency" had led to the arrest of 3,000 people and the destruction of 160 tons of books and other printed matter.

# More Recent Challenges

The ban against Burton's unexpurgated translation in any form other than the Worthington edition was not lifted until 1931, by the Tariff Act. However, a ban remained on another translation of *The Arabian Nights* by the French physician and translator Joseph Charles Mardrus. Since that time, expurgated versions of Burton's translation and others have filled the shelves of school and public libraries and made challenges to the rarer Burton original largely unnecessary.

One of the few recent reported cases of censorship took place in 1985 in Cairo, Egypt. Judge Ahmed el-Hossainy approved the confiscation of 3,000 copies of an unexpurgated edition of the work by the Ministry of the Interior on the grounds that it contained obscene passages that threatened the nation's moral fabric. He fined two booksellers and the book's publisher about $600 each for violating Egypt's pornography laws. "The book is not part of our heritage," stated Brigadier Adley el-Kosheiry, head of the morals department of the Ministry of the Interior. "But even if it were, any part of our heritage which included dirty words should be locked up in a museum and an expurgated version should be made available to youth."

Egypt's intellectuals and writers opposed the banning and saw it as a sign of the growing influence of Islamic fundamentalists in their nation. "If we continue to censor and eliminate obscene words from our literature, it will not stop there," warned Anis Mansour, a former editor of the Arabic journal *October*.

# Further Reading

"Cairo, Egypt." *Newsletter on Intellectual Freedom*, July 1985: 120.
"Comstock Not Yet Enlightened." *New York Times*, May 26, 1894: 5.
Haight, Anne Lyon, and Chandler B. Grannis. *Banned Books: 387 B.C. to 1978 A.D.* New York: R. R. Bowker, 1978.
Heins, Marjorie. *Not in Front of the Children: "Indecency," Censorship, and the Innocence of Youth.* New York: Hill and Wang, 2001.
Karolides, Nicholas J., Margaret Bald, and Dawn B. Sova. *120 Banned Books: Censorship Histories of World Literature.* New York: Facts On File, 2005.
McLynn, Frank. *Burton: Snow Upon the Desert.* London: John Murray, 1990.

Sova, Dawn B. *Banned Books: Literature Suppressed on Sexual Grounds.* New York: Facts On File, 2006.

## About the Translator of *The Arabian Nights*

### Sir Richard Francis Burton (1821–1890)

The original author (or authors) of *The Arabian Nights* is unknown. The various tales were told orally beginning in the eighth century and passed down from generation to generation. Most of the tales were collected into their present form in the thirteenth century, although additions were made as late as the sixteenth century.

French Orientalist and archaeologist Antoine Galland made the first known European translation, which was published from 1704 to 1712. Galland removed most of the sexual content from *The Arabian Nights,* making the stories appropriate reading for children.

The work was later translated into English by Jonathan Scott, Henry Torrens, and William Lane. The book swiftly became a great success. Western readers found the stories highly entertaining but were equally fascinated by the background of the life and culture of the mysterious East, which they previously knew little about. The most famous English translation, one that itself became a literary classic, was written by the English explorer, author, and linguist Sir Richard Francis Burton in 16 volumes between 1885 and 1888.

Burton was born on March 19, 1821, in Hertfordshire, England. A man of restless energy and curiosity, he joined the East India Company, a trading firm, in 1842 and moved to India. During his years there he mastered the Arabic, Hindustani, Persian, and Afghan languages. In his lifetime Burton learned 40 languages and dialects. In 1853 he traveled to the Arabian cities of Mecca and Medina, disguised as an Arab. (Westerners were forbidden at the time to enter these holy cities of the religion of Islam.) Burton's vivid account of his journey, published in 1855, was highly praised and established his literary reputation.

The following year Burton began his explorations of Africa in the company of fellow Englishman John Hanning Speke. In East Africa, Burton discovered Lake Tanganyika in 1858, while Speke discovered Lake Victoria. The two men later had a falling out. From 1861 onward, Burton served as British consul in West Africa;

Brazil; Damascus, Syria; and Trieste, Italy, where he spent the last 19 years of his life. He devoted most of his last years to his writing. While his translation of *The Arabian Nights* is his best-known work, he wrote more than 30 other books, mostly of his travels in exotic lands. Burton died of heart failure on October 20, 1890.

# Gulliver's Travels (1726)
## by Jonathan Swift

• • • • • • • • • • • • •

## What Happens in *Gulliver's Travels*

*Gulliver's Travels* is the tale of amazing adventures in remote countries among fantastical peoples, related in the first-person perspective by Lemuel Gulliver, a ship's surgeon. A satire of the world as seen through Swift's critical eye, *Gulliver's Travels* is written in the format of a travel narrative, which was an extremely popular literary genre in Swift's day.

In Book I Gulliver's ship is destroyed in a storm and he is washed ashore on an unknown island. He awakens from a deep sleep to find himself tightly bound to the shore by ropes. His captors are tiny people, six inches high, called Lilliputians. At first the Lilliputians are distrustful of this giant they call "Man Mountain." But gradually Gulliver earns their trust and helps them defeat their enemy, the people of the neighboring island of Blefuscu. Gulliver's sympathy for the Blefuscudians, however, turns the warlike Lilliputians against him. He flees Lilliput in a longboat and is eventually picked up by a ship out of Liverpool, England.

Book II recounts Gulliver's second voyage as a ship's surgeon. His ship anchors near an island, and Gulliver goes ashore with a small crew to find fresh water. The island of Brobdingnag is inhabited by a race of giants, one of whom captures Gulliver while the other crew members escape back to the ship. The man takes Gulliver to his farm, where his daughter, Glumdalclitch, cares for him with great kindness. But the farmer sees an opportunity to make money off tiny Gulliver and tours with him across the countryside. He then sells

Gulliver to the queen of Brobdingnag. Back at her palace, Gulliver meets the island's king, who debates the value of humankind, as explained by Gulliver. One day the large box that Gulliver calls home is snatched up by an eagle and dropped into the sea. He is again rescued by a passing ship and returns to England and his family.

In Book III Gulliver find himself promoted from ship's surgeon to captain of a sloop. While he is visiting islands for purposes of trade, pirates attack his sloop and set Gulliver adrift in a small boat. He comes across a flying island called Laputa, home to brilliant scientists and mathematicians who pursue such dubious tasks as extracting sunlight from a cucumber. The island below Laputa, Balnibarbi, is inhabited by a less technically advanced people who are the Laputans' sworn enemies. Gulliver eventually leaves these islands and reaches Japan, where he visits with the emperor and once again heads homeward.

Book IV finds Gulliver returning to sea as the captain of a merchant ship. He is again set upon by pirates, who instigate the crew to mutiny and leave Gulliver on a deserted isle. He is suddenly confronted by a race of ugly, hairy, humanlike creatures called Yahoos. Gulliver is rescued by a gray horse, a member of a superior and wise race of horses called Houyhnhnms (pronounced "winams"). He is greatly impressed by the Houyhnhnms and their civilization and wants to live among them for the rest of his days. However, the Houyhnhnms insist that Gulliver is a Yahoo, albeit an intelligent one, and must choose between living among the other Yahoos or returning to his own land. Sadly, Gulliver returns to England, where he sees his family and all other English people with new eyes. To him, they are all Yahoos, and he spends most of his time in his stables talking to his horses. The book ends with Gulliver an outcast among his own kind.

## Challenges and Censorship

"The chief end I propose to my self in all my labors is to vex the world rather than divert it," Jonathan Swift wrote to poet Alexander Pope in 1725 concerning his latest work, *Gulliver's Travels*. Despite Swift's intentions, this literary classic has diverted generations of young readers while often vexing their elders with its deeper and darker message that satirizes the folly of humankind. This has led to the book being expurgated—cleansed of all objectionable words and passages—more often than censored.

## Landmark Challenge: Early Attacks on Swift and *Gulliver's Travels*

As a satirist, Swift was used to having his writing misinterpreted by the public. His *Predictions for the Ensuing Year* was intended as a parody of a popular soothsayer, but it was taken literally by at least one Irish critic, who felt that "such uncanny prescience could not otherwise than signify collusion with the evil one himself."

The Roman Catholic Church saw all too well the implicit criticism of papists and religious dissenters in Swift's *A Tale of a Tub* (1704) and in 1734 put it on the Index, a list of officially forbidden literature that Catholics could not read without committing a sin. The papal ban was not lifted on the book until 1881, by Pope Leo XIII.

To avoid such censure of *The Drapier's Letters to the People of Ireland against Receiving Wood's Halfpence* (1724–25), Swift published these seven letters under the fictitious name M. B. Drapier, a shopkeeper "of Irish Stuffs and Silks." As Drapier, he attacked the British crown's granting William Wood a patent in July 1722 to coin copper for Irish currency without consulting the Irish Parliament. Swift/Drapier argued that the cheap copper money could easily be counterfeited and eventually ruin the Irish economy. The letters were so convincing that they motivated Wood to surrender his patent. While Swift's identity was never revealed, the printer of the letters, John Hood, and his wife, Sarah, were arrested and imprisoned. Swift wrote another letter, *Seasonable Advice*, in November 1724 that addressed the grand jury determining the Hoods' fate. Largely due to the letter, all charges were dropped against the couple.

*Gulliver's Travels* appeared two years later, and again Swift decided to have it published anonymously. He arrived in England with the manuscript in early 1726 and passed it around his circle of literary friends, who found it delightful. Pope urged Swift to demand 200 pounds for it from the London publisher Benjamin Motte, which he did. It was the only money Swift ever earned from his writing. He returned to his home in Ireland in August, and Pope dropped off the manuscript, author unknown, to Motte. "[H]e knew not whence, nor from whom, dropped at this house in the dark from a hackney coach," bubbled Pope.

The book was published in two volumes in October 1726, with several sections edited by Motte because he felt they were too sharply satirical to be accepted by the public. Swift was furious with the changes. "The whole Sting is taken out in several passages, in order to soften them," he complained to a friend. "Thus the Style is debased, the humor quite lost, and the matter insipid." Swift had the original passages put back in a 1734 edition.

The response to the book was overwhelmingly positive. The first printing sold out within a week, and the book was quickly translated into French, Dutch, and German. According to Pope it was "universally read, from the cabinet council to the nursery." Readers were captivated by Gulliver's imaginative adventures and Swift's sense of humor, largely missing the darker satire of humankind. Even fellow writers failed to see the deeper message. Poet John Arbuthnot called it "a merry work."

But some readers in positions of power were more perceptive. "The politicians to a man agree that it is fine from particular reflections," Pope wrote Swift, "but that the satire on general societies of men is too severe." Pope wrote a set of five *Verses on Gulliver's Travels* that Swift added to the second edition of his book.

It was not until the nineteenth century, more than 50 years after Swift's death, that the full savagery of his satire of modern civilization was fully recognized. Even as sophisticated a social critic as English novelist William Makepeace Thackeray was shocked by Swift's supposed misanthropy. In his *English Humorists of the Eighteenth Century* (1853), Thackeray called the book's moral "horrible, shameful, blasphemous filthy in word, filthy in thought" and believed Swift "about the most wretched being in God's world." Novelist Sir Walter Scott was slightly gentler in his criticism. Praising "the genuine spirit of satire of which it is made the vehicle," he nonetheless criticized the book for being "severe, unjust, and degrading."

Other writers defended *Gulliver's Travels*. Essayist William Hazlitt clearly saw Swift's goal to "strip empty pride and grandeur" and "to show men what they are, and to teach them what they ought to be."

The main problem for many readers lay in the second half of *Gulliver's Travels*. In fact, the first two books have often been published alone, carefully expurgated of all sexual and scatological (having to do with bodily functions) details, as children's storybooks. But while Gulliver's adventures among the Lilliputians and the Brobdingnagians could be enjoyed as pure adventure, it was difficult to overlook the implicit satire of books III and IV. Novelist Edmund Gosse condemned the "horrible foulness" of Book IV and urged all "decent" people not to read it. In 1882 writer Leslie Stephens blamed the "oppressive" tone of "misanthropy" in the last two books as a direct result of Swift's declining health and his bitterness over his frustrated political ambitions. He recommended that the public stop reading *Gulliver's Travels* with Book II.

While most editions continued to include books III and IV, a number of them published through 1899 excised the revolt of the Lindalinians that concludes Book III, seeing it as symbolic of a possible Irish revolt against England, something that the author may well have intended.

## Landmark Challenge: Gulliver in Pakistan

In the twentieth century, an abundance of abridged children's versions of *Gulliver's Travels* has reduced the number of challenges in schools and libraries. More recently, the book caused a stir in Pakistan at a higher institute of education. Lecturer Shahbaz Arif, at Punjab University in eastern Pakistan, included *Gulliver's Travels* on a list of objectionable works for university students in April 2003. "There are so many vulgar words, concepts, and thoughts reflected in the current curriculum of B.A. and M.A. literature that can influence our youngsters," he said. "There is a need to choose good literature to replace this bad one."

Among the other English classics on Arif's list were Alexander Pope's satirical epic poem "The Rape of the Lock," Henry Fielding's novel *Joseph Andrews,* and John Donne's metaphysical poetry. The censorship took on a deeper significance when it was learned that Arif was working under the orders of university Registrar Masud-ul Haq, a former army colonel, and Professor Nausheen Jamshed, of the Department of English Language and Literature. Jamshed is the wife of a former major general and a close friend of Sehba Musharaf, wife of former Pakistani President Pervez Musharaf.

The response from Pakistan's intelligentsia was swift and sharp. "It is enough to be ruled by cocksure generals," wrote *Friday Times* editor Najam Sethi. "Now we are to be taught English language and literature by their cocky wives."

"The list is not only ludicrous, it shows a spectacular lack of his own [Arif's] understanding of literature," said Waqqar Gillani of the *Daily Times*.

Professor Jamshed responded with indignation and innocence. "The press is unnecessarily dragging me and the first lady into this issue," she said. "The first lady is an educated and enlightened person. She can't order censorship of literature."

## Further Reading

"Gulliver's Travels: Critical Overview." Notes on Novels, Answers.com. Available online: www.answers.com/topic/gullivers-travels-novel-6. Accessed June 15, 2007.

Haight, Anne Lyon, and Chandler B. Grannis. *Banned Books: 387 B.C. to 1978 A.D.* New York: R. R. Bowker, 1978.

Hunting, Robert. *Jonathan Swift*. Boston: Twayne Publishers, 1967.

Karolides, Nicholas J. *Banned Books: Literature Suppressed on Political Grounds*. New York: Facts On File, 2006

"Lahore, Pakistan." *Newsletter on Intellectual Freedom,* November 2003: 231. Available online: https://members.ala.org/nif/v52n6/dateline. html.

Van Doren, Carl, editor. *The Portable Swift*. New York: Viking Penguin, 1977.

## About the Author of *Gulliver's Travels*

### Jonathan Swift (1667–1745)

Jonathan Swift is generally considered the greatest satirist in the English language, and *Gulliver's Travels* is universally regarded as his masterpiece. Swift was born in Dublin, Ireland, on November 30, 1667, to English parents. He attended Trinity College in Dublin and moved to England in 1689. For the next 10 years, Swift was the personal secretary to retired statesman Sir William Temple. During that time, he became a minister in the Church of England and met Esther Johnson, whom he called Stella. She became his lifelong friend and correspondent, and there is some evidence that they may have been secretly married. His *Journal to Stella*, consisting of his letters to her, was published posthumously.

In 1699 Swift returned to Ireland to become the pastor of a small parish. He traveled to England in 1703, and the following year published two of his best-known satires, *A Tale of a Tub* and *The Battle of the Books,* which respectively lampooned organized religion and literature. Swift's efforts as a spokesman and pamphlet writer for the English Tory government led Queen Anne to reward him by making him dean, or head clergyman, of St. Patrick's Cathedral in Dublin in 1713. He remained in that post for the remainder of his life. There he wrote *Gulliver's Travels* (1726) and his next-best-known work, the devastating essay "A Modest Proposal" (1729). In this savage satire he proposed that poor Irish families sell their babies to the English to be cooked and eaten.

Swift's health declined in his later years, and he died on October 19, 1745. While some critics called him a misanthrope who, like Gulliver, came to hate humankind, Swift claimed, "I have ever hated all Nations, professions, and Communityes and all my love is toward individuals." His goal in his writings, he said, was not to persuade people to give up on life but to work harder to make it better.

# Oliver Twist (1838)
## by Charles Dickens

• • • • • • • • • • • • • •

## What Happens in *Oliver Twist*

*Oliver Twist* is the story of a helpless orphan who survives many struggles to finally claim his rightful place in the world. Oliver's mother dies after giving birth to him in a workhouse. Having no known father, the child is put in a juvenile home, where he is mistreated. Nine years later, he is returned to the workhouse, where his plea for more food is severely punished. Oliver is apprenticed to the cruel undertaker Sowerberry. Flogged for disobedience, the boy runs away and goes to London.

He meets up with John Dawkins, also known as the Artful Dodger, a pickpocket. Dawkins brings him into a gang of young criminals led by the adult Fagin. During a pickpocketing, Oliver is arrested while the two real thieves get away. A witness clears the boy of the crime, and the victim, Mr. Brownlow, takes him home. Brownlow sees a strange resemblance between Oliver and the portrait of a young woman, his late daughter, in his house. He later learns Oliver is her child. But before that happens, Brownlow sends Oliver on an errand to test his honesty. The unfortunate youth is set upon by Fagin's accomplice Nancy and her boyfriend, the brutal Bill Sikes. Back in Fagin's lair, Oliver is sent out with Sikes to commit a burglary. The crime goes bad, and Oliver is wounded and left behind by Sikes and his cohorts.

Fagin is visited by the mysterious Mr. Monks, who has paid Fagin to make a criminal out of Oliver. Monks, it is later discovered, is Oliver's half brother, who wants to discredit him in order to gain Oliver's rightful inheritance. Nancy overhears their plot and, through an intermediary, tells it to Mr. Brownlow. When Fagin learns of her betrayal, he tells Sikes, who murders Nancy. Monk finally confesses his plot, and Oliver is reinstated. Sikes, while trying to escape the police, slips on a rooftop and accidentally hangs himself. Fagin is arrested and sentenced to hang. Oliver gains his inheritance and is adopted by the kindly Mr. Brownlow, who, it turns out, is his grandfather.

## Challenges and Censorship

*Oliver Twist,* published in 1838, was Charles Dickens's second novel and the first that he published under his real name. (He had previously published under the pen name Boz.) This engrossing tale of a young orphan boy, victimized by the heartless institutions of British society and the criminal underworld, helped to make Dickens famous. One of his most popular and most widely read novels, it has been successfully adapted into plays, movies, and a hit musical in 1960.

Despite all this success, the shadow of censorship has fallen over *Oliver Twist* more than any other of Dickens's 20 novels. His stereotypical depiction of the villain Fagin, who is Jewish, has led to charges of anti-Semitism ever since the book was first published.

## Landmark Challenge: The Problem of Fagin

Some early reviewers of the novel criticized Dickens for including criminals and prostitutes as major characters. "I saw no reason, when I wrote this book," Dickens responded, "why the very dregs of life, so long as their speech did not offend the ear, should not serve the purpose of a moral, at least as well as its froth and cream."

But it was one criminal character in particular that has over the years caused controversy and brought charges of anti-Semitism against the author. Fagin, the leader of the criminal gang that Oliver gets drawn into, is depicted by the author as an anti-Jewish stereotype. Fagin has a hooked nose, a long gabardine coat, and a reddish beard that makes him look like Lucifer himself. In one passage Dickens describes Fagin as "some loathsome reptile." In the original novel he refers to the character hundreds of times as "the Jew."

Anti-Semitism was a fact of life in England, as it was in much of Europe, when Dickens was writing his novel. Laws forbade Jews from entering respectable professions, forcing many to become moneylenders (a profession once forbidden to Christians) and buyers and sellers of old clothing, which is Fagin's "cover" profession for his nefarious criminal dealings. While Dickens was a product of his times, he was probably not particularly or consciously anti-Semitic.

But criticism that he was an anti-Semite rankled the author. When a Jewish woman wrote him and denounced his depiction of Fagin, he wrote back that "Fagin is a Jew because it unfortunately was true, of the time to which the story refers, that class of criminal almost invariably was a Jew."

While Dickens's future novels won praise from the public for his scathing depictions of poverty and injustice among the working class, the anti-Semitism of *Oliver Twist* was not forgotten. In 1860 Dickens, now a world-famous author, sold his home, Tavistock House, to a Jewish banker, J. P. Davis, whom Dickens privately referred to as "a Jewish Money-Lender." Dickens expected Davis to drive a hard bargain, but Davis was in fact fair and straightforward, dispelling the author's prejudices. "The bargain was made in five minutes . . . and the money paid within as many days," he wrote. Three years later, Dickens received a critical letter from Davis's wife, Eliza, who took him to task for his depiction of Fagin. She accused him of a "great wrong" against the "Jewish people."

"[I]f there be any general feeling on the part of the intelligent Jewish people that I have done them what you describe as 'a great wrong,'" responded Dickens, "they are a far less sensible, a far less just, and a far less good-tempered people than I have always supposed them to be." Fagin, he insisted, was historically accurate, "because he is one of the Jewish people, and because it conveys that kind of idea of him which I should give my readers of a Chinaman by calling him Chinese . . . I have no feelings toward the Jewish people but a friendly one. I always speak well of them, whether in public or in private."

Despite his defensiveness, Dickens must have felt a certain guilt about being labeled by some as an anti-Semite. To counter this, he created the good Jew Riah, in his last completed novel, *Our Mutual Friend* (1864–65). In an interesting reversal, Riah is forced to be the confederate of the Christian moneylender and slum landlord Fascination Fledgeby. Eliza Davis read the book and, in a grateful gesture, sent Dickens a new Hebrew-English Bible.

"There is nothing but good will left between me and a People for whom I have a real regard," wrote Dickens in reply, "and to whom I would not willfully have given an offence or done an injustice for any worldly consideration. Believe me."

Dickens went on to revise the text of *Oliver Twist* for a new edition of his works published in 1867 and 1868. He changed many of the Fagin references from "the Jew" to simply "Fagin" or "he." But Fagin was still Jewish and still a villain, albeit a colorful one. He remained a bone of contention for Jewish people in the twentieth century, when anti-Semitism reached the height of horror in the concentration camps of Nazi Germany.

## Landmark Challenge: Rosenberg v. Board of Education of the City of New York

In 1949 a group of Jewish parents in Brooklyn, New York, challenged the use of both *Oliver Twist* and William Shakespeare's play *The Merchant of Venice* in senior high school literature classes. *The Merchant of Venice* featured another "evil" Jew, Shylock, a moneylender who hates Christians and tries to extract a pound of flesh from the unfortunate title character. The parents declared that their children's rights to receive an education free of religious bias had been violated, leading them to sue the New York City Board of Education.

Both books should be banned from the school system, argued the parents, "because they tend to engender hatred of the Jew as a person and as a race." Murray B. Rosenberg, the group's leader, claimed the two books were "anti-Semitic and anti-religious" and "inimical to the best interests of growing children."

The case, entitled Rosenberg v. Board of Education of the City of New York, went to the Kings County Supreme Court, where it was heard by Justice Anthony J. DiGiovanna, who weighed the arguments carefully. "Public interest in a free and democratic society does not warrant or encourage the suppression of any book at the whim of any unduly sensitive person or group of persons," declared Justice DiGiovanna, "merely because a character described in such book as belonging to a particular race or religion is portrayed in a derogatory or offensive manner."

Furthermore, DiGiovanna held, a book could be suppressed only if it was shown to be "maliciously written for the apparent purpose of promoting and fomenting a bigoted and intolerant hatred against a particular racial or religious group." In DiGiovanna's opinion, neither work in question filled that description. He felt the removal of the books from the schools would not end the anti-religious feelings charged by the parents. He even believed that "removal may lead to misguided reading and unwarranted influences by the unguided pupil." The board of education, the court ruled, "acted in good faith without malice or prejudice and in the best interests of the school system entrusted to their care and control, and, therefore . . . no substantial reason exists which compels the suppression of the two books under consideration."

The way to fight intolerance, the judge believed, was with education at home and school, not with censorship. "Public education and instruction in the home will remove religious and racial intolerance more effectively than censorship and suppression of literary works which have been accepted as works of art and which are not per se propaganda against or for any race." Case closed.

## More Recent Challenges

In 1948, the year before the Brooklyn case, a film adaptation of *Oliver Twist* was released. The British movie was directed with tremendous flair and atmosphere by David Lean and starred actor Alec Guinness as Fagin. Guinness's Fagin was a mirror image of Dickens's creation. Hidden under pounds of makeup, the actor looked like a stereotypical Jew, with a hooked nose and lots of scraggly facial hair. English Jews protested the film and Guinness's portrayal, comparing it to the cruel caricatures the Nazis published in their newspaper *Der Stürmer* during the 1930s and 1940s. American critics were just as appalled by the perceived anti-Semitism of the film, which was not shown in the United States until 1951, with seven minutes of Fagin edited out. Guinness's performance can be seen as controversial, but he also brought a humor and humanity to Fagin that worked against the stereotype.

While *Oliver Twist* has continued to be challenged and banned in schools and school libraries since the 1950s, there have been far fewer challenges made against it than for most of the other books in this volume. Most readers have apparently followed the advice of critic Irving Howe, who wrote, "There is nothing to 'do' [about

Fagin] but confront the historical realities of our culture, and all that it has thrown up from its unsavory depths."

In an interesting reversal in 1978, the trustees of the Anaheim, California, Union High School District, in the words of the Secondary Teachers' Association, "banned thousands of books from the English classrooms." Among them were all the works of Dickens, with one exception—*Oliver Twist*.

## Further Reading

Ackroyd, Peter. *Dickens*. New York: Harper Collins, 1990.
"Educators Upheld in Book Freedom." *New York Times*, October 12, 1949: 31.
Kaplan, Fred. *Dickens: A Biography*. New York: William Morrow, 1988.
Karolides, Nicholas J., Margaret Bald, and Dawn B. Sova. *120 Banned Books: Censorship Histories of World Literature*. New York: Facts On File, 2005.
Mankowitz, Wolf. *Dickens of London*. New York: Macmillan, 1976.
"Notable First Amendment Court Cases." American Library Association (ALA) website. Available online: www.ala.org/ala/oif/firstamendment/courtcases/courtcases.htm. Accessed June 14, 2007.
Wilson, Angus. *The World of Charles Dickens*. New York: Viking, 1970.

## About the Author of *Oliver Twist*

### Charles Dickens (1812–1870)

Considered among the greatest of English novelists, Charles Dickens created a gallery of characters so real, they seem to have a life of their own apart from the novels that they appear in. Few authors of any age have been as read and beloved as Dickens.

Charles John Huffam Dickens was born on February 7, 1812, in Portsmouth, on England's southern coast. His father, John, was a poor clerk with the navy and moved the family to London when Charles was two years old. The family struggled in poverty, with John Dickens spending time in debtors' prison. When he was 12, Charles went to work in a factory pasting labels on bottles of shoe polish. That dreadful experience inspired him when he wrote his books.

After doing several other jobs, Dickens became a newspaper reporter, covering debates in Parliament for the London *Evening Chronicle*. The work taught him how to write quickly and concisely.

He published his first book, *Sketches by Boz,* a collection of his newspaper features, in 1836. That same year he married Catherine Hogarth, with whom he had 10 children. It was not a happy marriage: Catherine was intellectually her husband's inferior. The couple separated in 1858.

By then Dickens was the most renowned author in England and one of the most celebrated men of his time. His 20 novels include *David Copperfield* (1849–50), his most autobiographical novel; *A Tale of Two Cities* (1859), a historical novel about the French Revolution; and *Great Expectations* (1860–61), considered by many to be his greatest work.

A man of tireless energy, Dickens also edited two weekly magazines for many years (*Household Words* and *All the Year Round*), and was a brilliant dramatic reader of his works. His exhaustive reading tours of England and the United States, in which he strenuously played the parts of all his characters, undoubtedly contributed to his early death. Dickens suffered a stroke while writing his last novel, *The Mystery of Edwin Drood,* and died on June 9, 1870. He was buried in the Poets' Corner of Westminster Abbey. The inscription on his tomb reads: "He was a sympathiser to the poor, the suffering, and the oppressed, and by his death, one of England's greatest writers is lost to the world."

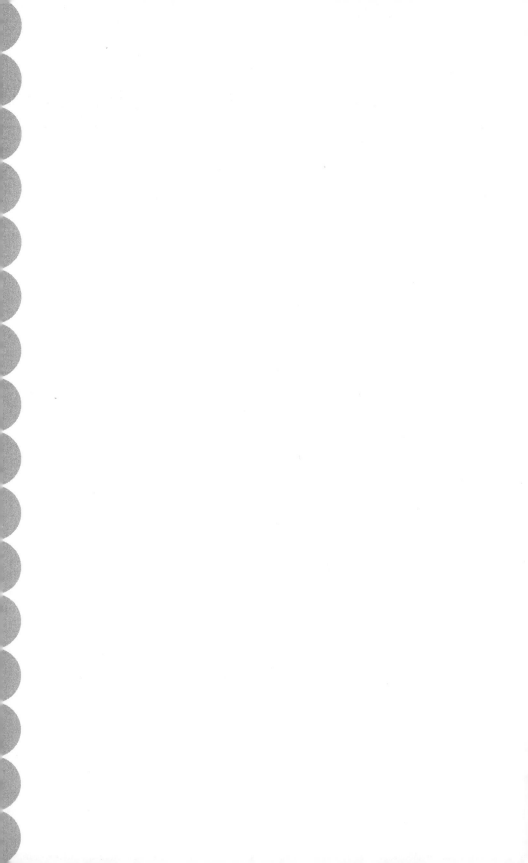

# The Adventures
# of Tom Sawyer (1876)
## by Mark Twain

. . . . . . . . . . . . .

## What Happens in *The Adventures of Tom Sawyer*

*The Adventures of Tom Sawyer* is Mark Twain's fond, somewhat romanticized, but never sentimental fictional look back at his childhood growing up along the Mississippi River in Hannibal, Missouri, some years before the Civil War. Tom Sawyer, the central character, is a good-hearted, imaginative, and mischievous boy who lives with his Aunt Polly. When Tom gets into a fight with a boy from St. Louis, he returns home with dirty clothes. Aunt Polly is horrified and punishes him by making him whitewash the fence around their home on Saturday, his day to play with his friends.

In one of the novel's most celebrated passages, Tom convinces his friends that whitewashing the fence is not work to him but something he'd rather do more than anything else. He is so persuasive that one by one, the other boys offer him gifts for the privilege of whitewashing the fence. He accepts their gifts and gets them to do his Saturday chore for him. Later that eventful day, Tom meets his new neighbor, the pretty Becky Thatcher, and falls hopelessly in love with her.

On Monday, on his way to school, Tom meets his friend Huckleberry Finn, son of the town drunk. Huck, because of his neglectful father, is the most independent boy in town and never goes to school. Tom agrees to meet him at midnight in the town cemetery to bury a dead cat. When Tom finally arrives at school, he is late. The teacher punishes him by making him sit in the "girls' section." Tom finds the punishment very bearable when he is seated next to Becky. She begins to warm up to Tom.

Later that night, Huck and Tom meet in the cemetery and find they are not alone. Dr. Robinson is there with two disreputable characters, Injun Joe and Muff Potter, who are digging up a recently buried corpse at the doctor's direction. The three have an argument and Muff is knocked out. Injun Joe then murders the doctor and plants the murder weapon by the unconscious Muff. Tom and Huck, terrified of being discovered, flee and vow never to reveal what they have seen. The next day, the doctor's body is discovered and Muff Potter is arrested and charged with his murder.

With school dismissed after the discovery of the murder, Tom, Huck, and their friend Joe Harper sail a raft to Jackson's Island in the river and stay there for days playing pirates, fishing, and smoking. The boys are reported missing and presumed drowned. When a funeral service is held for them, they sneak into the church and march down the aisle.

Back in school, Tom takes the blame for a minor misdeed of Becky's and suffers the punishment. This wins him Becky's heart. While Tom doesn't mind accepting blame for something he didn't do, his conscience won't let him stand by and watch Muff Potter be condemned to death for a crime he did not commit. He reveals the real murderer at Muff's trial, and Injun Joe makes his escape through an open window in the courthouse. Later Tom and Huck come upon Injun Joe and a cohort in an old abandoned house. The criminals have discovered a cache of gold coins, which they take to their hideout.

Becky's birthday is celebrated at a picnic, where some of the children decide to explore McDougal's Cave. Tom and Becky wander off by themselves and soon become lost in the vastness of the cave. About the same time, Huck follows Injun Joe and his partner as they head for the home of the Widow Douglas. He overhears Injun Joe reveal his intentions of injuring the widow in revenge for her late husband, Judge Douglas, who once publicly horsewhipped him. Huck tells a neighbor, Mr. Jones, of the plot, and Jones drives off the two villains.

Meanwhile, Tom and Becky, still lost in the cave, are the object of a massive manhunt. Tired and starving, the young people spot Injun Joe in the cave. After three days, Tom finally finds a way out of the cave and they are rescued. After recovering from their ordeal, Tom tells the townspeople that he saw Injun Joe in the cave. Another manhunt is conducted and Injun Joe, who could not find a way out of the cave, is found dead.

Tom and Huck return to the cave and discover Injun Joe's cache of gold coins, which are worth about $12,000. The money is invested for them, and the Widow Douglas adopts Huck, hoping to "civilize" him. But Huck has no intentions of changing his wayward ways; instead he runs away, setting the scene for a sequel to this novel, *The Adventures of Huckleberry Finn.*

## Challenges and Censorship

*The Adventures of Tom Sawyer* was a labor of love for Mark Twain— and he labored on it, off and on, for nearly five years. In this, his second novel, Twain relived his childhood in Hannibal, Missouri. He based Tom on himself; his girlfriend, Becky Thatcher, on a neighbor, Laura Hawkins; and his friend Huckleberry Finn on Tom Blankenship, the son of Hannibal's town drunk.

A children's classic, *Tom Sawyer* has often been paired in challenges with its sequel, *The Adventures of Huckleberry Finn*. Both books have been frequently challenged for their low humor, rough language, and racial slurs.

## Landmark Challenge: A Problematic Children's Classic

At one point in the writing of his novel, Twain considered taking Tom Sawyer into manhood, but later wisely abandoned the idea. Followed to adulthood, he wrote in a letter, "he [Tom] would just be like all the one-horse men in literature, and the reader would conceive a hearty contempt for him." Nevertheless he emphatically stated, "It is *not* a boy's book at all. It will only be read by adults." Twain's good friend, the critic and novelist William Dean Howells, disagreed after reading the finished manuscript. "It's altogether the best boy's story I ever read," he wrote. "It will be an immediate success."

Twain listened to Howells and decided *Tom Sawyer* was indeed better aimed at a youthful audience. To make sure it was worthy as such, he edited out "various obscenities" from the manuscript. In one instance, when Huck Finn complained that "they combed me all to hell" at the Widow Douglas's, Twain changed "hell" to "thunder."

The book was published first in England in June 1876 and in the United States in December 1876. Despite Howells's glowing prediction, the novel was not an immediate success. After a year, only 27,000 copies had been sold, far fewer than earlier Twain books such as *Roughing It*. Part of the lag in sales was due to a pirated edition printed in Canada. This cheap copy sold well on both sides of the U.S.–Canadian border, hurting sales of the legitimate U.S. edition.

The initial reviews of *Tom Sawyer* were generally good but rather shallow. A number of critics did recognize that the book's lack of "morbid sentimentality" and dulling moralizing heralded a new day in literature about and for children. "The story is a wonderful study of the boy-mind," wrote Howells in a review in the *Atlantic Monthly*, "which inhabits a world quite distinct from that in which he is bodily present with his elders, and in this lies its great charm and its universality, for boy nature, however human nature varies, is the same everywhere."

The *New York Times* critic had decidedly mixed feelings about *Tom Sawyer*. On the one hand, he was favorably impressed by the book's down-to-earth humor and lack of pretension, but he also felt the characters set a questionable example for young readers. "[I]t is not desirable that in real life we should familiarize our children with those of their age who are lawless or dare-devils," the reviewer wrote.

Some librarians felt more strongly about the book's negative models. The Brooklyn Public Library in New York City banned the novel from its children's room the year it was published. The Denver Public Library in Colorado removed all copies from both the adult and children's departments.

Sales of the book improved with the publication, in 1885, of *The Adventures of Huckleberry Finn*. A darker, more serious work, *Huckleberry Finn* created a demand for the earlier book and the two became closely linked in the public mind. By the same token, the censorship that overtook *Huck Finn* in the twentieth century also threatened *Tom Sawyer*, particularly due to the use of the word "nigger" in both books to describe blacks.

# Landmark Challenge:
# A Racially Divided School District

In November 1990, David Perry, the first black city council member of Plano, Texas, requested that the Plano Independent School District remove *Tom Sawyer* and *Huckleberry Finn* from the seventh- and eighth-grade reading lists. The following month, 600 concerned residents attended a school board meeting to consider the books' removal.

Among the more than 70 individuals who spoke at the meeting, support for and opposition to the books was largely divided along racial lines. Most blacks who spoke didn't want Twain's books taught. "Just to hear that word [nigger] has a searing and degrading and horrible effect on black people, especially our children," said Councilman Perry.

"Mark Twain frankly meant to offend people when he wrote *Huckleberry Finn,*" countered Bettye Mischen, a coordinator for English, speech, and journalism. "He wrote it to attack the attitudes of white politicians and white people who had negative attitudes about blacks."

Plano High senior Joanne Savage, who organized a petition signed by more than 500 students to retain the books in the curriculum, agreed. "To remove the book [*Huckleberry Finn*] from the taught reading in the curriculum would be a step in the wrong direction," she said. "The book has the ability to provoke much thoughtful discussion about this problem instead of ignoring it and pretending it doesn't exist."

But there were African-American students who opposed the novels. "You don't know how it feels to get in a classroom of twenty-some-odd people, being the minority, and having people look at you and wondering, 'Is he going to get offended by the word in this book?'" said senior Demarcus Smith.

In the end, the board ruled that seventh-graders could read *Tom Sawyer* and eleventh-graders could read *Huckleberry Finn.* Any students opposed to reading either book were allowed to read an alternate literary work.

## More Recent Challenges

The appropriateness of Twain's two boy novels for younger children was again raised in Columbus, Indiana, in February 1997. A group of 20 African-American residents led by the Reverend Charles Sims appeared at a meeting of the Bartholomew Consolidated School Corporation Board to speak out against the use of the novels in the curriculum of Columbus North High School. Reading either book,

Sims declared, was "degrading, insensitive, and oppressive" to African-American students.

A dialogue ensued between the board and community members, lasting a year. Finally the school administration suggested restricting the teaching of the books. A letter from English department chair Shirley Lyster was presented at a March 1997 school board meeting opposing this recommendation. "Teachers make sensitive and difficult decisions in writing curriculum and in selecting books," she wrote. "They are the professionals whose knowledge and skills afford them the trust of the corporation and the community."

Trying to balance the two sides on this delicate issue, the assistant superintendent for curriculum and instruction struck a compromise. She suggested that high school students could opt to take a class in which *Huckleberry Finn* would be read and taught, while middle school students could choose a class teaching *Tom Sawyer,* but only an edited version of the novel with the racially charged language omitted. Any student who did not want to deal with issues of racism in reading and discussion could take another class with alternative readings, she added.

In Burleson, Texas, *Tom Sawyer* was caught in the middle of a rigid policy that came under close scrutiny in 1998. A policy in place required all high school teachers to make parents aware of any book being read in class that contained profanity; such notification needed to occur within the first 14 days of each semester. Parents and teachers wanting to salvage *Tom Sawyer* and Harper Lee's *To Kill a Mockingbird,* among other books, spoke out against the policy.

In October of that year school trustees rescinded the policy and passed a new policy that would still require teachers to inform parents at the start of a semester of lists of reading material but would not have to detail any profanity. This compromise kept both conservative Christians and more liberal parents and teachers content. "We had two passionate sides," explained school Superintendent Fred Rauschuber, "and we were able to get them together and work out a happy medium that satisfied both of them."

Such compromises may well have brought a smile to the lips of Mark Twain and his alter ego, the often uncompromising Tom Sawyer.

# Further Reading

"Burleson, Texas." *Newsletter on Intellectual Freedom,* January 1998: 29.

"Columbus, Indiana." *Newsletter on Intellectual Freedom,* July 1997: 97–98.

Hoffman, Andrew. *Inventing Mark Twain: The Lives of Samuel Langhorne Clemens.* New York: William Morrow, 1997.

Powers, Ron. *Mark Twain: A Life.* New York: Free Press, 2005.

"Plano, Texas." *Newsletter on Intellectual Freedom,* March 1991: 45–46.

Sova, Dawn B. *Banned Books: Literature Suppressed on Social Grounds.* New York: Facts On File, 2006.

Ward, Geoffrey C., Dayton Duncan, Ken Burns, and Russell Banks. *Mark Twain: An Illustrated Biography.* New York: Alfred A. Knopf, 2001.

Ziff, Larzer. *Mark Twain.* New York: Oxford University Press, 2004.

# About the Author of
# *The Adventures of Tom Sawyer*

### Mark Twain (1835–1910)

Samuel Langhorne Clemens, better known as Mark Twain, is considered one of the greatest of American authors. He was born on November 30, 1835, in Florida, Missouri, and grew up in the town of Hannibal, on the Mississippi River. The river would play a major role in a number of his works, including *Tom Sawyer* (1876) and *Huckleberry Finn* (1885). His father, a failed lawyer and storekeeper, died when Twain was 12. He went to work at an early age for his older brother Orion, who published a newspaper in Hannibal. Twain later moved east and worked for four years as a traveling typesetter.

Eventually Twain returned to his first love, the Mississippi, and became a steamboat pilot. It was during this time that he first heard the boatman's term "mark twain," to describe a water depth of 2 fathoms, or 12 feet. He would later make it his pen name. Twain worked the river as a pilot until the Civil War broke out in 1861 and shut down all trade on the Mississippi.

Later that year, Orion was appointed secretary of the new territory of Nevada, and Twain traveled there with him by stagecoach. He got a job as a reporter in Virginia City, Nevada, and soon after wrote the short story that made him famous, "The Celebrated Jumping

Frog of Calaveras County" (1865). Twain's use of colorful American dialect in this and other humorous stories was something new in American literature.

In 1869 Twain published his first book, *Innocents Abroad,* which told of his adventures on a tour of Europe and the Holy Land taken two years earlier. The success of this book led him to marry Olivia Langdon, the heiress of a wealthy New York family, in 1870. The couple settled in Hartford, Connecticut, the following year, where Twain wrote a string of successful books, including *The Adventures of Tom Sawyer* (1876), *A Tramp Abroad* (1880), and *Life on The Mississippi* (1883). He completed *The Adventures of Huckleberry Finn* in 1883 after working on it, off and on, for seven years.

In 1891 Twain left Hartford and spent nine years of self-exile in Europe. During this time he made a successful around-the-world lecture tour, which recouped huge losses he had suffered in unwise investments. His later works are savagely satirical of American society and deeply pessimistic about the future of civilization. In his final decade Twain was one of the most popular authors in the world and, in his own words, "the most conspicuous person on the planet." He died in Redding, Connecticut, on April 21, 1910.

# The Adventures of Huckleberry Finn (1885)
## by Mark Twain

### What Happens in
### *The Adventures of Huckleberry Finn*

*The Adventures of Huckleberry Finn* follows the further escapades of Huckleberry Finn, a rambunctious 15-year-old boy who first appeared in Twain's earlier book *The Adventures of Tom Sawyer* (1876). As the story opens, Huck, who narrates the novel, is living with the Widow Douglas and her sister, Miss Watson, two older women who are trying, despite his resistance, to "civilize" him. Huck recounts his adventures with his friend Tom Sawyer and their discovery of $12,000 in a cave.

When Pap Finn, Huck's dissolute father, learns of the wealth that Huck now possesses, he kidnaps him and holds him hostage in a remote cabin across the Mississippi River on the Illinois shore. Subjected to savage beatings by his father, Huck devises a plan to escape. He fakes his own murder and flees to Jackson's Island on the Mississippi. Here he meets up with Miss Watson's runaway slave, Jim. Both Huck and Jim are looking for a better, freer existence, and they form a strong bond of friendship. Jim plans to get to the town of Cairo, Illinois, and from there travel on the Ohio River north to the free states. Although he likes Jim, Huck's conscience is troubled by the fact that he is abetting a runaway slave. He struggles with this issue of slavery throughout the novel.

The two find an abandoned raft on the island and travel down the river on it. They hide on land during the day and travel on the raft by night. One night their journey is interrupted when a steamboat strikes their raft and rips it in two. Huck swims to shore and is separated from Jim. He is taken in by the Grangerfords, an eccentric Southern family who are fighting a blood feud with their neighbors, the Shepherdsons. Jim finds Huck and the two watch as members of the feuding families kill one another, one by one. They finally go back to the river and resume their journey.

Next they meet up with two confidence men, the Duke and the Dauphin, who commandeer their raft. They stop at one river town after another and carry out their confidence scams on the residents. The Duke and the Dauphin finally embroil Huck in their plot to deceive a family out of its inheritance by posing as two English brothers. The real brothers show up, exposing their scam, and Huck and Jim manage to escape, but the Duke and the Dauphin catch up with them. Needing money, the two con men sell Jim back into slavery to Silas and Sally Phelps, who are Tom Sawyer's uncle and aunt.

Huck goes to the Phelps farm, where he is mistaken for Tom. The real Tom shows up and goes along with the charade, posing as his brother, Sid. Together they plot to free Jim from his new masters. Tom dismisses Huck's straightforward and practical plan in favor of his own elaborate plan of escape that involves snakes and secret messages. After several aborted attempts, they succeed in freeing Jim, but while making their getaway, Tom is shot in the leg by a farmer. Jim, the most morally upright character in the novel, risks recapture to nurse Tom until his leg is healed. Jim is returned to the farm, where Tom reveals what he knew all along—that Miss Watson, who has died, freed Jim in her will. Jim is free to go his own way and Huck decides to do the same. Fed up with the wicked ways of civilization, he resists Tom's aunt's wish to adopt him and "lights out for the territory" and presumably more adventures.

## Challenges and Censorship

Today considered one of the greatest of American novels, *The Adventures of Huckleberry Finn* is also one of the most controversial. It is that rare classic American novel that straddles the worlds of both adult and children's literature, making it the target of attacks from parents, teachers, school administrators, and librarians for more than a century. Challenges have largely been based on three factors: the roughness of Huck's language, the supposed vulgarity of much of the action, and the racial slurs, especially the word "nigger," directed at Jim the runaway slave.

# Landmark Challenge:
## *Huck*'s "Low Grade of Morality"

"I shall *like* it, whether anybody else does or not," Mark Twain wrote on completing the novel in the summer of 1883. And it seemed for a time that almost nobody else, or at least no serious critics, *would* like it. Even before *The Adventures of Huckleberry Finn* was published in book form, it was a topic of censorship. Twain had allowed *Century* magazine to excerpt sections of his new novel, a standard practice at the time. *Century* editor Richard Watson Gilder was unhappy with Twain's coarse language and his references to such taboo topics as a person's nakedness and dead cats. He removed all such offensive references before publication.

Perhaps sensing the difficulties he would face with finding a publisher for his book, Twain decided to publish it himself. *Huck Finn* was published in early 1885 by Charles L. Webster and Company of New York, headed by Twain's nephew. Among the other works to come from Twain's press that year was the two-volume *Personal Memoirs of U. S. Grant,* which became a best seller and saved the former president from bankruptcy.

Unlike the reviews for Grant's memoir, those for *Huckleberry Finn* were not encouraging. Reviewers criticized the crudity of the narrative and dialogue, the coarseness of Huck's character and behavior, and the low moral stature of many of the other characters. Ironically, the author had taken great pains to remove anything that he thought would be objectionable to his readers. He had his friend, novelist and critic William Dean Howells, go over the manuscript carefully, and he threw out several proposed illustrations that he found too "violent" or "disgusting."

The most crushing blow for Twain, however, came in March 1885, when the public library in Concord, Massachusetts, the cradle of American literature and home to Ralph Waldo Emerson and Henry David Thoreau, banned the book from its shelves. The Concord Library Committee had originally approved the book without reading it, "knowing the author's reputation." But the "learned librarian" read it with displeasure, leading the committee to read the book carefully and come to the same conclusion.

"It deals with a series of adventures of a very low grade of morality," the committee members wrote. They found it "flippant," "irreverent," but, curiously "contain[ing] but very little humor." Louisa May Alcott, author of *Little Women* and one of Concord's leading literary lights, wrote, "If Mr. Clemens cannot think of something better to tell our pure-minded lads and lasses, he had better stop writing for them."

In response to such attacks, Twain claimed, albeit tongue in cheek, that he had never intended his book for children. "I wrote *Tom Sawyer* and *Huck Finn* for adults exclusively, and it always distresses me when I find that boys and girls have been allowed access to them," he declared when the book was banned by the Brooklyn Public Library in New York. "The mind that becomes soiled in youth can never again be washed clean. I know this by my own experience, and to this day I cherish an unappeasable bitterness against the unfaithful guardians of my young life, who not only permitted but compelled me to read an unexpurgated Bible through before I was fifteen years old." Twain's sarcasm, as in his novel, undoubtedly went unrecognized by many of his critics.

But not everyone got on the bandwagon to ban *Huck Finn*. There were numerous librarians and newspaper writers who recognized it for the fine work it was. *The San Francisco Chronicle* called the Concord banning "absurd." "There is a large class of people," it said, "who are impervious to a joke, even when told by as consummate a master of the art of narration as Mark Twain. For all these the book will be dreary, flat, stale, and unprofitable. But for the great body of readers it will furnish much hearty, wholesome laughter."

This prediction quickly proved accurate. *Huck Finn* was largely shunned by the critical establishment yet embraced by the general public. Twain acknowledged this and the debt that he owed the people who banned his book in a letter to the secretary of the Concord Free Trade Club, which had elected him a member of their organization. "[A] committee of the public library of your town have condemned and excommunicated my last book and doubled its sale," he wrote. "This generous action of theirs must necessarily benefit me in one or two additional ways. For instance, it will deter other libraries from buying the book; and you are doubtless aware that one book in a public library prevents the sale of a sure ten and a possible hundred of its mates. And, secondly, it will cause the purchasers of the book to read it, out of curiosity, instead of merely intending to do so, after the usual way of the world and library committees; and then they will discover, to my great advantage and their own indignant disappointment, that there is nothing objectionable in the book after all."

*Huckleberry Finn* remained a controversial book to the end of its author's life in 1910. A *Library Journal* article of 1907, "The Children's Librarian versus Huckleberry Finn," claimed that the novel had been banned somewhere in the country ever since its publication.

As the twentieth century progressed, however, critical opinion began to shift, and Twain's novel was eventually recognized as a great work of literature. Esteemed critic Lionel Trilling acknowledged that the book banners had a point, as he found the novel a truly "subversive book." But, Trilling noted, Huck, in his thoughts and actions, rejects everything about the society of his day—including its bigotry, intolerance, violence, decadence, and corruption. By mid-century, *Huckleberry Finn* was required or recommended reading on high school reading lists across the nation.

## Landmark Challenge: The "N" Word

By the 1960s, the assaults on *Huckleberry Finn* in school districts were largely focused on its frequent use of the word "nigger" by Huck and other characters. Twain's use of the explosive racial slur was faithful to the pre–Civil War South, of which his native Missouri was a part. But responsible African-American parents protested his use of it, claiming it demeaned their schoolchildren, made them uncomfortable, and robbed them of self-esteem.

To satisfy the protesters and keep the book in the curriculum, several textbook publishers omitted the "n" word or found substitutes for it. Scott Foresman of Chicago rewrote entire passages to eliminate the word, while others replaced it with "slave" (Singer) or "servant" (McGraw-Hill). Only Ginn & Company of Boston, Massachusetts, had the courage to stay true to Twain's writing and retain the word, reinforcing its decision with an essay by Lionel Trilling, who gave reasons why it should remain in the work.

Meanwhile, across the country, school boards were caving in to pressure from African-American parents and organizations. In 1992 the superintendent of the Kinston, North Carolina, school district removed the book from the middle school curriculum, claiming students were too young to be exposed to the word "nigger." The following year, the Carlisle, Pennsylvania, school superintendent declared the word and other racial slurs demeaning to all students—black and white.

But not all school boards gave in to parental pressure. In February 1997 the Reverend Charles Sims and 20 members of the African-American community in Columbus, Indiana, attended a school board meeting and called for the removal of both *The Adventures of Tom Sawyer* and *The Adventures of Huckleberry Finn* from the high school curriculum. Sims claimed that the books were "degrading, insensitive, and oppressive." When all 17 high school English teachers and their department chair supported continuing to teach the books, the assistant superintendent told the group, "Nobody is taking *Huck Finn* off the shelves."

Other school systems have tried to educate their students by putting the book in historical context. In 1996 the novel was removed from classes in Cherry Hill, New Jersey, and then reinstated a year later. The new curriculum taught the novel in the context of the era when it was written, in order to give students a deeper understanding of Twain's motives and the racial views of his times. The curriculum was developed by Villanova University professors who offered a required half-day training session to all teachers who opted to teach the novel.

If Mark Twain were alive today, he probably would have been more saddened than amused by these challenges. In truth, Twain was among the least racist writers of his day. In one letter he wrote that "the shame is ours" regarding racism against blacks and that "we should pay for it." He intended *Huckleberry Finn* in part as a savage satire that condemned slavery and racism as inhumane. However, the novel was still a product of its time. Some modern writers, such as Ralph Ellison, author of *Invisible Man* (1952), have been sharply critical of the depiction of Jim in the novel.

## Landmark Challenge: One Student's Campaign

One of the most publicized challenges of the novel in recent years occurred in Portland, Oregon, in the fall of 2002. Johnnie Williams Jr., an African-American junior at Lincoln High School, complained that he was uncomfortable reading *Huck Finn* in his American literature class. Lincoln High School was predominantly white; at the time, only 5 percent of the student body was African American.

The administration allowed Williams to read an alternative book, a biography of black baseball legend Jackie Robinson. But Williams's mother, Angela Scott, wouldn't let the matter drop there. She insisted that it was wrong for the school's English teachers to continue to teach the book, disregarding her son and other black students' feelings. She found an ally in Portland school board member Derry Jackson, who, at an October 14, 2002, board meeting, asked Superintendent of Schools Jim Scherzinger to find out in which classes and schools the novel was being assigned and then assess its appropriateness. Jackson was not supported by the rest of the school board, which felt that the complaint of one student was not grounds enough to call the book's appropriateness into question. "I suggest that we take this matter serious," Jackson countered. "Don't be quick to dismiss this as trivial."

Lincoln High Principal Peter Hamilton pointed out, in the English department's defense, that teachers were sensitive to the feelings of black students when they assigned the book. He pointed to supplemental materials used to put the novel in historical context and special sessions some teachers held with their African-American students to discuss issues raised by *Huck Finn*. Angela Scott was not impressed. "My question is: If you have to do all that, then why [read] the book?" she argued.

As the controversy continued, more black students came to Williams's defense. The Black Student Union at neighboring Franklin High School went to Lincoln and pressed students to sign petitions requesting that the Portland school board review the situation and the racial problems raised by classroom discussions of the book.

"I know that all teachers in the district are not prepared for the conversations that might come out of reading that book," said Black Student Union President Charles McGee, a junior who had read the book in his sophomore year and liked it. "Until we let students voice how they feel on an everyday basis, the board and the community really don't know. We want them to listen." McGee and his colleagues collected more than 200 signatures at Lincoln and three other Portland high schools.

*The Adventures of Huckleberry Finn* continues to be a controversial book in the classrooms of America and will probably remain so. In his book *Banned in the U.S.A.,* author Herbert N. Foerstel lists it as the second most-banned book in the nation as of 2002. The American Library Association ranked it fifth on its "100 Most Frequently Challenged Books of 1990–2000." As Twain scholar and Pulitzer Prize–winning author Justin Kaplan wrote in 1974: "The spirit of *Huckleberry Finn,* its intention, and indeed the entire difference between literature and propaganda may be no better understood now than they were in 1885."

## Further Reading

Foerstel, Herbert N. *Banned in the U.S.A.: A Reference Guide to Book Censorship in Schools and Public Libraries.* Westport, Conn.: Greenwood Press, 2002.

Hechinger, Fred M. "About Education: Irrationality, Futility and Huck's Censors." *New York Times,* June 4, 1985: C6.

Kaplan, Justin. "Born to Trouble: One Hundred Years of Huckleberry Finn." Washington, D.C.: Library of Congress, 1985.

_____. *Mark Twain and His World.* New York: Simon & Schuster, 1974.

Karolides, Nicholas J., Margaret Bald, and Dawn B. Sova. *120 Banned Books: Censorship Histories of World Literature.* New York: Facts On File, 2005.

"Portland, Oregon." *Newsletter on Intellectual Freedom,* January 2003. Available online: https://members.ala.org/nif/v52n1/censorship_dateline.html.

## About the Author of
## *The Adventures of Huckleberry Finn*

See biography in *The Adventures of Tom Sawyer* entry.

# Little Black Sambo (1899)
## by Helen Bannerman

● ● ● ● ● ● ● ● ● ● ● ●

### What Happens in *Little Black Sambo*

*Little Black Sambo* is the simple but appealing story of a little boy living in a jungle fantasyland that is a mixture of India and Africa. Sambo goes for a walk one day in the forest wearing a new red coat and blue trousers made by his mother, Black Mumbo, and a green umbrella and purple shoes bought by his father, Black Jumbo, at the bazaar.

He encounters four hungry tigers, one at a time, on his walk. To stop them from eating him, Sambo offers each tiger an article of clothing, which they readily accept. Finally, he is left wearing only a waistcloth. He heads home in tears, but then hears the tigers coming and hides behind a palm tree.

The four beasts begin to argue about which of them is the grandest tiger. The argument turns into a fight, and the tigers cast off their finery and begin to pursue one another around a tree. Faster and faster they run until the hot sun melts them into a pool of butter.

Black Jumbo appears on his way home from work and collects the butter into a big pot. Sambo is happy to have his clothes back and accompanies his father home. Once there, Black Mumbo uses the butter to fry up pancakes and the family sits down to eat a feast. Little Black Sambo devours 169 of the tiger-colored pancakes.

### Challenges and Censorship

*Little Black Sambo* holds a unique place in children's literature. Since first appearing in 1899, it has remained one of the most popular and beloved of all children's stories, told and retold countless times. Since the 1950s, it has also been the most controversial, the most challenged, and the most racially charged children's book in the English language.

A children's story written in 1899 by a woman whose husband was part of the British colonial empire might well be expected to be condescending toward ethnic peoples. And to a certain extent, the original *Little Black Sambo* is just that. Such obsoleteness might be put in historical perspective by modern readers, if not for two other unfortunate factors—the central character's name, which has strong racial overtones, and the subsequent illustrations of the story, which are racially charged.

## Landmark Challenges: The "S" Word

Helen Bannerman's text is quite charming and innocent, but the names she gave her three main characters are not. "Sambo" is derived from a word in the Hausa language of north Nigeria meaning "second son." It was a common name for male slaves in colonial times and, by 1806, according to language scholar Stuart Berg Flexner, was used by many whites when referring to any black man or boy.

"If you say 'sambo,' it's not as bad as 'nigga,' but it's certainly as bad as 'darkey' or to some extent, 'pickaninny,'" said David Pilgrim, curator of the Jim Crow Museum of Racist Memorabilia at Ferris State University in Big Rapids, Michigan. "How can you write a book whose central character has a name that you would not call a black person?"

As bad, if not worse, are the names Bannerman gave Sambo's parents—Black Mumbo and Black Jumbo. The names seem to mock the very culture and society of colonial peoples of color, whose language and customs to most Europeans were just a lot of "mumbo jumbo."

Then there are the pictures. Bannerman's original illustrations suggested an Indian setting. Sambo's clothing and home are definitely Indian, and tigers are native to India, not Africa. But she gave Sambo some distinctly African features—such as his kinky hair and dark brown skin. Yet Bannerman's illustrations are mild compared to those that were created for later editions, unapproved by her because she did not retain the copyright to the book. Many of the later Sambos are stark caricatures of Africans and African Americans. They have bulging eyes, thick rubbery lips, and plantation grins. While the United States remained a largely segregated society through the 1940s, Sambo's stereotypical image was rarely challenged. But when the civil rights movement accelerated in the 1950s, Americans' consciousness of these stereotypes was raised.

Sam Battistone and Newell Bohnett weren't thinking about Bannerman's book when they opened their first Sambo's restaurant in Santa Barbara, California, in 1957. The name was created by combining parts of the two men's names (Bohnett was known to everyone as "Bo"). But that changed when people began to associate the restaurant with the story and the owners decided to decorate the walls of their growing chain of restaurants with scenes from the story. By 1979 there were 1,200 Sambo's restaurants in 47 states. African-American organizations campaigned against the chain for its name and its alleged discrimination against the hiring and promoting of minority employees. The controversy and resulting lawsuits pushed the chain into bankruptcy in 1981. By the following year, only the original restaurant remained open. Today the Santa Barbara Sambo's is run by Battistone's grandson, Chad Stevens, who is attempting to rebuild the chain.

By 1963, a landmark year in the civil rights movement, the number of challenges against the book were numerous. Lincoln, Nebraska, School Superintendent Steven N. Watkins received a letter from the local human rights council complaining of the book's "inherent racism." Watkins promptly had all copies of the book removed from school library shelves. Watkins responded to defenders of the book saying it was "not worth making an issue over . . . There are plenty of good stories left." However, he later backpedaled on his decision and had the stored copies placed on the reserve shelf of each library. He had a note attached to each copy, stating while "not a part of the instructional program, it will be available to those who want to read it as optional material."

In 1971 parental complaints in Montgomery County, Maryland, led to the removal of not only all copies of the book from county school libraries, but also all filmstrips and records that retold the story of Sambo. A special committee of parents, librarians, teachers, and others found the work "not in keeping with good human relations" but also denied they were censoring the book. "[T]he decision is not to be construed as book burning, but rather as book selection," a committee spokesperson insisted.

Political commentator James J. Kilpatrick was incensed by the Maryland case. "This is baloney," Kilpatrick fumed on a radio broadcast. "In the ordinary sense of the metaphor, this is indeed book burning, pure and simple. It is a capitulation to pressure groups . . . And it is utterly futile. *Little Black Sambo* cannot be suppressed. It will continue to exist, a small classic of sorts, just as *Huckleberry Finn* and *Tom Sawyer* will continue to exist. Neither will this gesture improve race relations or enhance the pride and dignity of black children."

## Landmark Challenge: Sambo in Japan

While Sambo's star was waning in the United States and England, half a world away in Japan the book remained more popular than ever. *Chibikuro Sambo,* the Japanese version of the familiar tale, had remained a top-selling children's book since the 1950s and was adored by generations of Japanese children. Sambo dolls, with thick lips and bulging eyes, were a favorite toy.

Then in 1988, pressure from westerners who were offended by the story, including African Americans living in Japan, caused Japanese book publishers and manufacturers to stop printing the book and making the doll.

Many librarians, teachers, and parents were surprised and disappointed by the response. "It never occurred to me that the story encouraged anti-black prejudice," said Norishiga Fukushima, a Kyoto kindergarten teacher whose students annually performed a play based on the book. "The children identify with the heroic little Sambo. They experience the thrill as he overcomes one danger after another. It is a lovable tale."

"I feel sorry it will no longer be published because it has delighted so many Japanese children," said Katsuko Uchiyama, who works at one of Tokyo's largest bookstores. "I cannot see that it gives a bad impression of black people."

"We are sorry if anyone has been offended," said Hisao Ogawa, chief children's book editor for Iwanami Shoten, a publishing house that has sold more than a million copies of *Chibikuro Sambo.* "We saw it as a tale of a brave little boy. Japanese children have delighted in the tale of little Sambo for many, many years."

Other Japanese saw a more subtle prejudice at work. "Sambo and his family represent blacks under colonial rule," said Midori Fujita, an expert on African affairs. "Children reading the book may subconsciously get a wrong image of blacks."

"This society has an amazing lack of awareness of how certain stereotypes can hurt," said Mal Adams, an American television producer living in Tokyo. "I guess it [the banning of the book] is a positive move, as far as it goes. It shows Japan is becoming a little more sensitive."

## Landmark Challenge: The Repackaging of Sambo

Since the 1990s, Americans writers and illustrators have been finding new ways to repackage Bannerman's classic story to make it less objectionable. In 1996 African-American children's author Julius Lester and illustrator Jerry Pinkney retold the story, retitling it *Sam and the Tigers*. They set the tale in the fantasy country of Sam-sam-sa-mara and depicted Sam as a modern, realistic African-American youth. "This is a wonderful story," Lester said, but admits it has had a troubled history. "Very unconsciously, with no malice aforethought, [Bannerman] was reflecting her times. And the fact that she was hurting black people never entered her mind. Which doesn't let her off the hook."

The same year Lester and Pinkney's book came out, children's author and illustrator Fred Marcellino published his own version, *The Story of Little Babaji*, planting the setting and characters more firmly in India than even Helen Bannerman had.

Both books got good reviews and caused little controversy. Such could not be said of illustrator Christopher Bing's *The Story of Little Black Sambo*, published in 2003. Bing, who is white, had loved the story from childhood and used Bannerman's original text with his own illustrations. Controversy began to swirl around Bing's illustrations even before they were published. The public library in Lexington, Massachusetts, where Bing lives, put 15 of his *Sambo* drawings on display, prompting an objection from a parent. Then William D. Valentine, head of the Lexington Montessori School, wrote a letter to a leading local bookstore urging it not to offer Bing's book for sale.

Once published, the book was generally praised by critics. The *Kirkus Review* hailed it as "[a] handsome restoration of the classic story" and admired "the transformation of its original protagonist from a stereotype to a beautiful African child living in India." It was selected for the Kirkus 2003 Editor's Choice list along with 39 other children's books.

But others saw Bing's revision as another sad chapter in a racially questionable saga. "I don't see how I can get past the title and what it means," said Dr. Alvin F. Poussaint, director of the Media Center at the Judge Baker Children's Center in Boston. "It would be like trying to do 'Little Black Darky' and saying, 'as long as I fix up the character so he doesn't look like a darky on the plantation, it's OK.'"

"This was a labor of love; nothing more," insisted Bing. "It was never meant to offend. In fact, it was meant to do the opposite . . . I would love for the black community to be able to take this image and this original story and make it a positive."

The controversy over *Little Black Sambo*—the book in all its variations, the restaurant, the doll and other products—continues to this day. Unlike the fierce tigers who ran so fast that they turned into butter, the defenders and critics of *Little Black Sambo* look like they will continue to chase one another around and around with no end in sight.

# Further Reading

Bannerman, Helen. *Little Black Sambo.* New York: Harper Collins, 2003 [reprint].

Bannerman, Helen, and Christopher Bing, illustrator. *The Story of Little Black Sambo.* Brooklyn, N.Y.: Handprint Books, 2003.

"Ban on Sambo: Censorship or Socially Responsible Action?" *Newsletter on Intellectual Freedom,* September 1971: 119.

Daniel, Mac. "Lexington Artist Draws Sambo Story Under New Light." *Boston Globe,* October 8, 2003: B6.

Kennedy, Louise. "New Storybook Reopens Old Wounds." *Boston Globe,* December 14, 2003: A1.

LaMotte, Greg. "Sambo's Revival Running into Hot Water." CNN Interactive, January 28, 1998. Available online: www.cnn.com/US/9801/28/sambo.revival. Accessed June 19, 2007.

McGillis, Roderick. *Voices of the Other: Children's Literature and the Postcolonial Context.* New York: Garland, 1999.

Nickerson, Colin. "Japan's Sayonara to Black Sambo." *Boston Globe,* January 23, 1989: 2.

Sova, Dawn B. *Banned Books: Literature Suppressed on Social Grounds.* New York: Facts On File, 2006.

## About the Author of *Little Black Sambo*

### Helen Bannerman (1863–1946)

Helen Bannerman was born Brodie Cowan Watson in Edinburgh, Scotland, in 1863, the daughter of a Scottish minister. As a young woman of her time, she was not allowed to receive a degree from a British university. Instead, she studied and took exams at the University of St. Andrew in Edinburgh and received a special L.L.A. degree (Lady Literate in Arts).

In 1889 she married William Burney Bannerman, a surgeon in the Indian Medical Service. The couple moved to India, then a colony of Great Britain, where they remained for 30 years. They lived in Madras, a southern city with an unhealthy climate. Many people there, especially children, contracted serious tropical diseases. The Bannermans, who had two daughters, sent their children to live part of the year with a nanny in the town of Kodaikanal in the hill country. Helen remained during this time with her husband, but regularly made the two-day rail journey to Kodaikanal to visit her daughters.

On one such train trip in 1899, Bannerman whiled away the time writing and illustrating a story about a young Indian boy named Little Black Sambo to share with her daughters. The girls loved the story, as did Bannerman's friend Alice Bond. Bond persuaded Bannerman to let her take the story to London, England, where she hoped to find someone to publish it. Bond was offered five pounds for the book's copyright by London publisher Grant Richards. Afraid to wait for another offer, she accepted without consulting with Bannerman, who had hoped to retain the copyright.

*The Story of Little Black Sambo* was an immediate best seller. Bannerman's way with a story, her repetitive sentences, and her unrefined but appealing illustrations were all innovations in children's books. Her central character, it is believed, was the first black hero in a children's story. Unfortunately, because she did not own the copyright, other publishers came out with their own unauthorized editions, often with new illustrations. These illustrations and the sometimes altered text turned Sambo and his parents into ugly caricatures of Africans that brought charges of racism, much to Bannerman's shock and regret.

She wrote a number of other books with Indian settings and characters, including *The Story of Little Black Mingo* (1901), *Pat and the Spider* (1905), *The Teasing Monkey* (1907), and a sequel to her first book, *Sambo and the Twins* (1936).

Bannerman died in 1946. She claimed to the end of her life that she never intended to offend black people or anyone else with her children's books. "My mother would not have published the book had she dreamt for a moment that even one small boy would have been made unhappy thereby," her son Robert wrote in a letter to the *London Times* in 1972.

# The *Little House* Books
# (1935–1943)
## by Laura Ingalls Wilder

• • • • • • • • • • • • •

## What Happens in the *Little House* Books

The *Little House* series chronicles the childhood of Laura Ingalls Wilder, who grew up with her family in the pioneering days of the Midwest during the late nineteenth century. There are eight books in the series; the best-known and third in sequence is *Little House on the Prairie*.

*Little House on the Prairie* begins with the family moving from their home in the Big Woods of Wisconsin to Indian Territory in Kansas. Once there, Pa Ingalls builds a house for his wife, daughter Laura, and her sisters Mary and baby Carrie. Various challenges befall the Ingalls, including a bout of the dreaded disease malaria, which nearly kills the entire family. Dr. Tan, an African-American physician who works among the Indians, brings the Ingalls back to health. Another intriguing character who befriends the Ingalls is Mr. Edwards from Tennessee, who gives the girls Christmas presents that he brought all the way from Independence, Kansas. As the book ends, the government informs Pa Ingalls that all homesteaders must leave Indian Territory to avoid conflicts with the Indians. Rather than wait to be forced off his land by the military, Pa moves out and again takes to the road with his family, their destination unknown.

In the next two books in the series, *On the Banks of Plum Creek* (1937) and *By the Shores of Silver Lake* (1939), Laura grows into adolescence. In *The Long Winter* (1940), the Ingalls women are trapped indoors during snowstorms and nearly starve to death. Finally Laura grows into young womanhood in *Little Town on the Prairie* (1941) and *These Happy Golden Years* (1943).

## Challenges and Censorship

Perhaps no children's book series, until the appearance of *Harry Potter*, has been as beloved and praised as Laura Ingalls Wilder's *Little House* books. Generations of young readers have cherished these books, which were the inspiration for the popular television series *Little House on the Prairie*, which ran from 1974 to 1983 on the NBC network.

The idea that the *Little House* books could be challenged and removed from classrooms and school libraries was unthinkable before the 1990s. Only then did some people see Wilder's ambivalent attitude toward one particular group of people as questionable, if not offensive. These people were the Native Americans who cohabited the prairie where young Laura and her pioneer family lived.

## Landmark Challenges: Indians in the House

Most of the challenges have centered on the third and most popular book in the series, *Little House on the Prairie* (1935), whose working title was *Indian Country*. In the chapter "Indians in the House," two warriors invade the family's home while Pa Ingalls is away. They steal some of Pa's tobacco and order Ma to make them cornbread. The author describes the Indians as wearing bad-smelling skunk pelts. The violation of the settlers' home is shocking, and the fear felt by six-year-old Laura and her sister Mary is palpable.

In 1993 these details deeply offended Houma Indian Brenda Pitre in Thibodaux, Louisiana, as she read the book, taken out from the school library, to her third-grade son. She was also deeply troubled when another character says, "The only good Indian is a dead Indian."

"I thought about the many children who read this book and weren't as fortunate as my son was to have somebody guide them through the book and explain what was being said and the time period it involved," said Pitre. " . . . A book that would portray Indians this way would do no good at all for a child's self-esteem." She urged school officials at a Lafourche Parish school system committee meeting to remove the book from elementary school libraries and classrooms, but saw no reason why it could not be taught in middle or high schools.

Committee member Nancy Powell noted that the novel's character Pa Ingalls rejects the harsh statement about Indians made by Mrs. Scott, a neighbor who hates and fears Indians. In many passages, Powell pointed out, Indians are shown in a positive light. While librarian Jeanette Reed Robideux admitted that the author was not always sensitive to Native Americans, she said this had to be put in historical perspective. "Laura Ingalls Wilder wrote that a long time ago and perhaps she was not as sensitive as we would like to be about those things," Robideux said. "I don't think we would accept that from a contemporary writer writing today."

In the end, the committee rejected Pitre's request and kept the book in the school libraries to reflect different views and times. "We can't just pull things out because we disapprove," said Thibodaux Elementary School librarian Jo Carpenter.

In 1998 Angela Cavender Wilson, a Sioux living near Granite Falls, Minnesota, requested that *Little House on the Prairie* be removed from the third-grade curriculum when her eight-year-old daughter came home from Yellow Medicine East Elementary School "visibly upset" after reading the statement "The only good Indian is a dead Indian."

Wilson visited the school and talked to students about the book's racism and the rich Dakota heritage of her family. When she appeared before the school board with her complaints in October of that year, the board agreed to appoint a committee to review the book. In the meantime, the title was temporarily removed from the curriculum.

The matter came to the attention of the Minnesota Civil Liberties Union (MCLU), which sent a letter in December to the board ordering that the book be returned to schools. "The idea that bad ideas ought to be censored is unconstitutional," wrote MCLU Executive Director Charles Samuelson. School Superintendent Bob Vaadeland would not back down from the board's decision, however, until the committee had returned from its review and a new policy for book challenges could be formulated.

In her perceptive study of the *Little House* books, Ann Romines notes that the scene of the Indians' invasion in *Little House on the Prairie* is the author's "attempt to convey, from a white girl's viewpoint to a readership of children, the extraordinary stresses and tensions that burdened even the simplest contact between Euro-

American females and Indian men." She counters the two warriors in this chapter with the friendly Osage who appears later in the novel, known as Soldat du Chene. This intelligent Indian leader speaks French and becomes the family's protector. It is he who leads the Osage past the Ingalls' home in a migratory march. But in the end, it is the United States government that forces the Ingalls family to leave Indian Territory and find another home.

Like many settlers of his time, Pa believes in the pervading nineteenth-century philosophy of Manifest Destiny. In a deeply revealing scene in *Little House on the Prairie,* he tells Laura, "When white settlers come into a country, the Indians have to move on . . . That's why we're here, Laura. White people are going to settle all this country, and we get the best land because we got here first and take our pick. Now do you understand?" "But, Pa," his daughter replies, "I thought this was Indian Territory. Won't it make the Indians mad to have to—." But Pa refuses to answer any more questions and tells Laura to "go to sleep."

"Wilder believed that the complexity and the tragedy [of settlers vs. Indians] were not beyond the comprehension of young children," wrote children's author and editor Elizabeth Segel.

## Landmark Challenge: The Wrong Song

It is not only Wilder's depiction of Native Americans that has brought challenges to her books in schools. In 1996 in Stockton, California, African-American parent Claudia Thurman complained about a racial slur against blacks in *Little House in the Big Woods.* A teacher at the Village Oaks Elementary School was reading from the book to her son's third-grade class and came upon a song sung by Pa that mentions "Old Uncle Ned" who has "gone where the good darkeys go."

In response to the challenge, a library council committee voted to remove the book from the third-grade literature list but retain it on the school library shelf. This half-measure was unacceptable to Thurman. "Each individual child who's been taught this kind of negativity at home can go and find this book in the library," she said. "[This decision] does not take the book out of the school system . . . I'm not stopping here. There is more we need to do. I want it out of the library, and there are other books like this out there."

Thurman found strong support from the organization Parents of African-American Students. "They're pacifying us," declared the group's president, Denrick Robertson. "They're taking it off the list, but they're still leaving it for kids to read. It's still there. This is promoting racist epithets [terms of abuse]. It's fueling the fire of racism."

On November 26, in a 3 to 0 vote, the trustees of the Lincoln Unified School District not only refused to remove the book from the school library but also rejected the committee's recommendation to take it out of the classroom. "This is not a racist book," insisted board member Don Riggio. "There's this one chapter where a father sings a song that is inappropriate by today's standards. They can read the book without that chapter."

Janet Ghio, chairperson of Lincoln High School's English Department, argued to the trustees that the library council committee's decision was not based on a thorough investigation. While she thought challenges such as Thurman's were healthy and helped put things in perspective, she was strongly opposed to banning controversial literature.

As scholar Ann Romines has pointed out, the first major African-American character to appear in the series is the well-educated, professional Dr. Tan, whom Wilder based on a real person who had lived near Independence, Kansas. Dr. Tan not only serves the health needs of the Indians but also saves the Ingalls family from death when they contract malaria. Even the Ingalls' Indian-hating neighbor Mrs. Scott has nothing bad to say about Dr. Tan.

# Further Reading

"Granite Falls, Minnesota." *Newsletter on Intellectual Freedom,* March 1999: 36.

Romines, Ann. *Constructing the Little House: Gender, Culture, and Laura Ingalls Wilder.* Amherst, Mass.: University of Massachusetts Press, 1997.

Sova, Dawn B. *Banned Books: Literature Suppressed on Social Grounds.* New York: Facts On File, 2006.

"Stockton, California." *Newsletter on Intellectual Freedom,* January 1997: 9; March 1997: 50.

"Thibodaux, Louisiana." *Newsletter on Intellectual Freedom,* July 1993: 125–126.

# About the Author of the *Little House* Books

## Laura Ingalls Wilder (1867–1957)

Laura Ingalls was born on February 7, 1867, near Pepin, Wisconsin, in the "Big Woods" that she wrote about in the first two volumes of her popular children's series. She was the second of five children. The family moved frequently during Laura's early years, living in Kansas's Indian Territory, Missouri, Iowa, and finally settling down near De Smet, a frontier town in Dakota Territory in 1879.

At age 15, Laura became a schoolteacher, but she left that profession when she married homesteader Almanzo Wilder in 1885. The couple started a farm just north of De Smet and suffered many hardships over the next several years. Their second child, a son, died as a newborn; a fire consumed their house and barn; and a drought ruined their crops and drove them to leave the newly formed state of South Dakota in 1890.

After a brief time in Florida, where Laura found the humidity intolerable, they returned to De Smet and worked jobs in town to save toward another farm. In 1894 they moved to Mansfield, Missouri, and started a farm they called Rocky Ridge Farm. They continued to struggle financially until Almanzo's parents bought the deed to their rented house; they were soon able to move permanently to Rocky Ridge.

In 1911 Laura wrote an article for the *Missouri Ruralist,* which led to a full-time position writing a column called "As a Farm Woman Thinks," which she continued through the mid-1920s. Inspired by her daughter, Rose, a successful author in her own right, Laura began to write a children's book about her childhood memories called *Pioneer Girl.* Retitled *Little House in the Big Woods* (1932), it became the first of her eight *Little House* books, published over the next 11 years. The series became immensely popular and made Laura a famous and wealthy writer.

The Wilders continued to live at Rocky Ridge until Almanzo's death, at age 92, in 1949. Although Rose tried to convince her mother to come live with her at her home in Danbury, Connecticut, Laura remained at the farm. She died there on February 10, 1957, at age 90. Today, the farmhouse and adjoining stone cottage are a National Historic Landmark and museum.

In recent years, controversy has arisen over what role daughter Rose Wilder Lane played in the writing of the books. While some literary critics theorize she did most of the writing, a majority of critics feel that she helped her mother shape and edit the manuscripts while Laura did most of the original writing herself.

# *Of Mice and Men* (1937)
## by John Steinbeck

### What Happens in *Of Mice and Men*

*Of Mice and Men* is the simple, tragic story of George Milton and Lennie Small, two footloose men drifting from job to job in Depression-era California. George is intelligent and cunning, while Lennie is big, gentle, and mentally disabled. The two men, despite their differences, share a common dream of one day owning their own little ranch and never having to work for anyone else again. Lennie, who loves furry little animals, will tend the rabbits on their dream ranch.

The two friends land jobs at a large ranch where they meet Candy, an old-timer who offers them his life's savings to help buy the ranch and become a partner in their dream. George agrees to the bargain and predicts that in a month's time they can quit their jobs and buy the ranch they have longed for.

But there are complications. Curley, the no-account son of the ranch's owner, goads Lennie into a fight. Lennie refuses to defend himself, until George urges him to do so. Lennie breaks the bones in Curley's hand with his uncontrollable strength. Slim, another ranch hand, makes Curley promise not to get Lennie fired; he is to tell his family and other people on the ranch that his hand got caught in a machine. It is apparent, however, that Curley has it in for Lennie and will seek vengeance. Curley's attractive wife is a flirt, but the men know to stay away from her—all the men, that is, except simple-minded Lennie. While alone with her, Lennie is delighted when Curley's wife lets him stroke her hair. Lennie's touch is rough, however, and she tells him to stop. When she screams, Lennie panics and accidentally breaks her neck, killing her. He hides the body in the barn and flees to his hiding place in the woods. Candy and George find the body and immediately know that Lennie is responsible.

When Curley learns of his wife's death, he organizes the men to hunt down Lennie and lynch him. George manages to find Lennie in the woods before the lynching party does. Too saddened to chastise his friend, George tells Lennie to look off in the distance and picture their dream ranch, which they will now never own. As he does, George shoots him in the head, sparing him the horror of being lynched by the others. With Lennie dies the dream the two friends had so fervently pursued.

## Challenges and Censorship

Few novels have been staples of high school reading lists as long as *Of Mice and Men,* and few have been as frequently challenged by parents and community action groups or as often banned by school boards. Steinbeck's novel ranked in fourth place in author Herbert N. Foerstel's list of banned or challenged books from 1996 to 2000, and in sixth place in the American Library Association's "100 Most Frequently Challenged Books of 1990–2000."

The challenges lodged against *Of Mice and Men* have been based on a number of factors—vulgar or obscene language, racism, a mentally retarded central character, mercy killing, and an implicit critique of the American social system. In fact, the liberal political leanings of John Steinbeck are more muted in this work than in others, including his masterpiece, *The Grapes of Wrath.* Yet because of its brief length, clear-cut story line, and symbolism, *Of Mice and Men* is considered a perfect teachable modern novel and has suffered numerous challenges for its popularity with English departments across the nation.

## Landmark Challenge:
## A Superintendent Speaks Out

In 1988 parental complaints at White Chapel High School in Pine Bluff, Arkansas, about the profane language in *Of Mice and Men* led a committee of parents, teachers, and administrators to order it removed from the required reading list. Those teachers who still wanted to teach the novel continued to do so, offering an alternative title to students who were offended by the book.

As the 1988–89 school year began, more parents complained about the book. School Superintendent Charles "Danny" Knight decided to take action, immediately ordering the book banned from all classrooms and demanding that teachers turn in their school copies. Both teachers and students at White Chapel protested the banning, but Knight wouldn't budge.

"It's tough on a student to be the one person to raise his hand and say, 'My parents don't want me reading this book' when everybody else is reading it," Knight said. "And if a student does object, what happens when the book is being discussed? He has to go out into the hall with his other book. When does he get taught?"

The superintendent refused to view his actions as censorship. "We haven't banned the book," he insisted. "If it was banned, it wouldn't be on the library shelves available to any student who wants to read it. All we've done is respond to parents who objected to their children being required to read the book."

Some English teachers reacted sharply to Knight's directive. "My twelfth-graders are passionate about this," said Nancy Ward. "They read it two years ago and they're upset that it's not going to be taught." Referring to two other highly praised novels, Dell Wanda Gorman asked, "What do you think they'll say about *Ordinary People* or *The Great Gatsby*? There's no stopping once you've opened this can of worms."

## Landmark Challenge: One Father's Campaign

In 2000 Tom Mouw's daughter was reading *Of Mice and Men* in her tenth-grade English class at Grandville High School in Michigan. The novel had been a required part of the English curriculum at the school for 25 years. While his daughter said nothing about the book during the school year, she later told her parents that its raw language had upset her. Incensed that the school had never asked him for permission to teach his daughter this book, Tom Mouw decided to do something about it.

In March 2002 he submitted a formal "Citizen's Request for Reconsideration of Educational Material" to the school district. Several months later a review committee decided to overrule his complaint and keep Steinbeck's novel in the curriculum. Library media specialist Susan Tamm explained to Mouw, in a letter, that teachers were trained to carefully prepare students for the book's language and viewpoint and that a majority of students enjoyed the novel and the important themes it presented. Furthermore, she wrote, any student who was offended by the book could read an alternative book in its place.

Unsatisfied by this response, Mouw took his challenge on appeal to the school board. "The book is full of racism, profanity, and foul language," he wrote in his second letter. He reported that he and his wife had found some 200 profanities in the book, including swear words, racial slurs, and the taking of God's and Jesus' names in vain. "I would hope students at our high school are not allowed to call a black student a [racial slur] or a mentally slow student a nuisance or 'a dumb bastard,'" Mouw continued. "These phrases are typical throughout the book."

After some time, curriculum director Denise Seiler called Mouw to tell him his appeal had been denied. While Mouw's oldest daughter was being home-schooled, his two younger children still attended public schools. He said he planned to elect for them to read an alternative book when they reached the tenth grade. Despite the failure of his campaign against *Of Mice and Men,* he still would like to see the book removed from the classroom. "There are so many good books out there for our children to read," Mouw said. "It is time to get this one out of our schools."

## Landmark Challenge: Not "Normal" in Normal

A 2003 challenge in Normal, Illinois, was unusual because it focused on neither language, mental disability, nor violence, but racism. Normal Community High School sophomore Kayla Napue, who is black, said she felt degraded while the book was being taught in her English class. She was deeply disturbed by the racial slurs made by white characters in the novel against the sole black character, the stable hand Crooks. Napue left the classroom and went to the school library during the weeks the book was read and discussed.

The school suggested an alternative Steinbeck novel, *The Pearl,* for her, but Napue and her family rejected the offer. Her mother, Connie Tripp, also complained about negative racial language in two other books, *The Adventures of Huckleberry Finn* and *To Kill a Mockingbird,* and requested that they too be banned. "A lot of kids were supportive," said Napue of the challenge, "and it was not just African Americans."

Sue Cain, the educational chairperson of the local branch of the National Association for the Advancement of Colored People (NAACP) and a former teacher, did not recommend that the books be banned but suggested they did not give a balanced picture of society. "While these stories may contain a part of the African-American struggle," she said, "they by themselves are incomplete and become offensive if the story is not also told by those who have actually experienced this struggle." To fill out the picture, she suggested a number of titles by African-American authors to be included in the English curriculum.

A trio of white high school students spoke up in defense of Steinbeck's novel. "I feel very passionately about the book and its impact on me as a student," said Calli Grimes. "The language promotes change." Another student claimed that the book "offers insights into a difficult period in America's history."

The controversy continued through the school year, with the challengers stressing the reasonableness of their arguments. "We have never asked that these books be banned," declared Rozalind Hopgood of Bloomington. "We've asked that they be removed from the required reading list."

A diversity advisory committee made up of parents and community members recommended keeping *To Kill a Mockingbird* on the required reading list but offered the novel *The Chosen* as an alternative to *Huckleberry Finn* for those students who didn't want to read it. They held fast, however, on the banning of *Of Mice and Men*, claiming that it does not "address multicultural and socially sensitive issues in a meaningful, respectful manner."

Sue Cain of the NAACP endorsed the option for students to choose from books that share the same general theme. The diversity advisory committee also recommended classes in diversity and sensitivity training for teachers, along with "literary previews" to be made available to parents and students before each book is assigned in class. In addition, the committee endorsed read-along guides to be sent home to family members while a book is being read and studied.

*Of Mice and Men* will undoubtedly draw further challenges as it continues to hold a secure place on high school reading lists. Thomas

Scarseth, who teaches at the University of Wisconsin at La Crosse, explained its wide appeal by calling it "a teachable good book: simple and clear, yet profound and beautiful." The beauty comes from the book's affirmation of humankind and not its depiction of the down-fall. "In the last analysis," writes author Paul McCarthy in his study of Steinbeck, "George and Lennie symbolize something of the enduring and hopeful as well as the meaningless. They manage—if only for a brief time—to rise above circumstances and to convince others as well as themselves that dreams are part of the territory . . . ."

The effect of the novel on generations of readers is perhaps best summed up by steelworker Dave Jackson of Louisville, Ohio, who opposed the banning of the book in a local high school. "It's been over 30 years since I read the book," he said at a meeting of the board of education. "I can still remember the characters. I can still remember the storyline. I remember the feelings of compassion and sympathy for the mentally disabled. It changed my outlook on the mentally disabled. I don't remember the language in the book. I don't remember being offended."

# Further Reading

Foerstel, Herbert N. *Banned in the U.S.A.: A Reference Guide to Book Censorship in Schools and Public Libraries.* Westport, Conn.: Greenwood Press, 2002.

"Grandville, Michigan." *Newsletter on Intellectual Freedom,* November 2002: 280. Available online: https://members.ala.org/nif/v51n6/success_stories.html.

Karolides, Nicholas J., Margaret Bald, and Dawn B. Sova. *120 Banned Books: Censorship Histories of World Literature.* New York: Facts On File, 2005.

McCarthy, Paul. *John Steinbeck.* New York: Frederick Ungar, 1980.

"Normal, Illinois." *Newsletter on Intellectual Freedom,* January 2004: 11. Available online: https://members.ala.org/nif/v53n1/dateline.html.

"Normal, Illinois." *Newsletter on Intellectual Freedom,* September 2004: 177–78. https://members.ala.org/nif/v53n5/dateline.html.

"Pine Bluff, Arkansas." *Newsletter on Intellectual Freedom,* January 1990: 10.

Smith, Jack. "Are We of Mice or Men? Eternal Vigilance Is the Price of Freedom from Literary Censorship." *Los Angeles Times,* January 16, 1986: 1.

Young Adult Library Services Association. *Hit List: Frequently Challenged Books for Young Adults.* Chicago: American Library Association, 1996.

# About the Author of *Of Mice and Men*

### John Steinbeck (1902–1968)

John Steinbeck was one of the most popular American authors of the twentieth century. He was born on February 27, 1902, in Salinas, California, the setting of many of his novels and stories. His father was the county treasurer; his mother was a former schoolteacher who instilled in him a love of literature.

Steinbeck worked on ranches as a young man and studied marine biology at Stanford University in his home state. His first book, *Cup of Gold* (1929), was a novel about the life of pirate Henry Morgan. He gained critical success and fame with his novel *Tortilla Flat* (1935), about California migrant workers. Steinbeck first conceived of *Of Mice and Men* (1937) as a play, and it was dramatized and later adapted three times on film.

Steinbeck reached the peak of his writing career with *The Grapes of Wrath* (1939), a grimly realistic but humane account of the Joad family, farmers from Oklahoma who migrate to California looking for a better life during the Depression. It won him the Pulitzer Prize the following year. Steinbeck produced many books during the 1940s and 1950s, but none matched the critical success of *The Grapes of Wrath*.

In the 1940s he tried his hand at screenwriting and was nominated for an Academy Award for Best Story for *Lifeboat* (1944), directed by Alfred Hitchcock. In 1952 he produced what he felt was his best novel, the epic *East of Eden,* a story of a father and two brothers in the Salinas Valley that had heavy biblical overtones.

Steinbeck won the Nobel Prize for Literature in 1962. In his acceptance speech he said that "the writer is delegated to declare and to celebrate man's proven capacity for greatness of heart and spirit—for gallantry in defeat, for courage, compassion, and love." Steinbeck's deep compassion for the common, working people illuminated his best fiction. He published no new fiction after receiving the Nobel Prize and died of heart disease in New York City on December 20, 1968.

# *Black Boy* (1945)
## by Richard Wright

## What Happens in *Black Boy*

*Black Boy: A Record of Childhood and Youth,* published in 1945, is the harrowing story of writer Richard Wright's early years growing up black in the racist South. While it is based solidly on Wright's experiences, it is not strictly an autobiography. Wright admitted that he partly fictionalized his life to give it more dramatic impact, and the book reads more like a novel than an autobiography.

It starts with Richard, age four, setting fire to his grandmother's house in Jackson, Mississippi. His mother beats him severely for this act, but, as with so many other brutal experiences in his life, Richard survives it. The family moves to Memphis, Tennessee, to find new work opportunities, but instead Richard's father deserts them. In Memphis the growing boy learns about the racism of whites against blacks and how it degrades those closest to him.

The family moves back to Jackson to live with Richard's grandmother, whom he hates, while his mother gradually recovers from an illness. It is here that Richard starts to write stories and discovers writing to be an escape from both the black and white worlds from which he is increasingly alienated. By age 16 he has set his sights on becoming a professional writer. His only hope of achieving this dream, he feels, is in going north, where racism is less ingrained than in the South.

After graduating from high school, Richard steals money from an employer to go north, but he only gets as far as Memphis. He comes to regret his crime and desires to do good in the world in the future. While working at menial jobs in Memphis, he haunts the public library and devours novels and other books. In the novel's final pages, Richard finally has the means to flee to Chicago, Illinois, the city where he will fulfill his destiny and become a writer.

## Challenges and Censorship

Among African-American authors, few have been as frequently challenged in schools and libraries as Richard Wright. That fact speaks to the honesty, the power, and the relevance of Wright's work to an America that is still struggling with racism today.

Wright was unsparing in his depiction not only of Southern whites and their racist culture, but also of the twisted black lives—including his own—that were forever changed by that racism. The harsh realism of the language and violent behavior of the protagonist and others have instigated many of the challenges to *Black Boy* over the years.

## Landmark Challenge: Northern Censorship and Southern Racism

The problem of censorship began when the 37-year-old author first brought his finished manuscript for *Black Boy,* then called *American Hunger,* to his editor at Harper & Row, a major New York publisher. The book included Wright's experiences as a struggling writer in Chicago and New York City. When the manuscript was submitted to the panel of the Book-of-the-Month Club, it recommended that the last section, making up about a third of the total manuscript, be dropped. If Wright agreed to the change, which would end the book with him leaving the South, the panel would recommend the novel as a Book-of-the-Month Club selection, which could make it a best seller.

Wright accepted this decision but later regretted doing so. He felt that the panel of the Book-of-the-Month Club was uneasy with the last part of his novel, especially its depiction of northern racism and Wright's unflattering description of the workings of the American Communist Party, from which he subsequently resigned. Rightly or wrongly, he thought the panel, and possibly Harper & Row, did not want to offend the Soviet Union, a Communist country and a staunch ally of the U.S. in World War II, which was just ending.

For the rest of his life Wright tried but failed to get the final third of his book published. Only 30 years after his death was it finally published—under its original title, *American Hunger*. The following year *Black Boy* and *American Hunger* were published as one book, as Richard Wright had originally intended.

Like his earlier novel *Native Son*, *Black Boy* enjoyed good sales, boosted by its status as a Book-of-the-Month Club selection. But its popularity did not extend to the Deep South, where Wright's descriptions of racism were met with denial and anger. The book was banned in Mississippi, where much of *Black Boy* takes place.

Mississippi Senator Theodore Bilbo, a staunch segregationist and white supremacist, condemned the book on the floor of the U.S. Senate, calling it "a damnable lie, from beginning to end . . . The purpose of the book was to plant seeds of hate and devilment in the minds of every American. It was the dirtiest, filthiest, most obscene, filthy and dirty, and came from a Negro from whom one could not expect better."

While challenges regarding racial hatred continued to be voiced, by the 1970s most challenges focused on, at least on the surface, the book's profanity and indecent, antisocial behavior.

# Landmark Challenge:
# From School Board to Supreme Court

A 1975 challenge in a school district on Long Island, New York, led to a case that over a period of seven years went all the way to the U.S. Supreme Court and ended in a landmark decision on the censorship of books in schools and school libraries.

On the night of November 7, 1975, two members of the school board of the Island Trees Union Free School District No. 26, in Levittown, New York, asked the high school janitor to let them into the school library. Their mission: to find out how many items on a list of "objectionable" books the library had on its shelves. The list had been provided to the board two months earlier by a community action group, the Parents of New York United (PONY-U). Going through the card catalog, the men found nine books from the list. These included *Black Boy* and *Best Short Stories by Negro Writers*, edited by black poet Langston Hughes. There were also two Pulitzer

Prize–winning novels on the list—Oliver La Farge's *Laughing Boy* and Bernard Malamud's *The Fixer.*

The following February, the seven-member school board invited two high school principals in the district to their regular meeting. They showed them excerpts from the nine objectionable books provided by PONY-U and then ordered them to remove the books from the library shelves. Eventually two more books on the list were found and added to those to be removed.

When the school superintendent objected to the book banning without a formal review and hearing, the school board ordered him to remove "*all* copies of the library books" at once. A grievance filed by the local teachers' union—claiming the action violated their contract and threatening action from the New York Civil Liberties Union—did not faze the school board. At a press conference the group held on March 19, 1976, they retaliated: "Does the news media decide from which books your children are taught? Should it be the people who award the Pulitzer Prizes? Or, maybe it should be today's dedicated teacher union leaders? We believe that not even the professional educators and educational administrators have a right to [take away] the parents' authority . . . God help all of us if the parents should ever lose their authority."

Pressure to remove the books continued to grow. On March 30 the board agreed to appoint eight people to a committee to review the books. They included a recent high school graduate, a high school principal, a former PTA president, and a local mailman. After several months of deliberations, the review committee made its recommendations. It suggested that *Black Boy, Best Short Stories by Negro Writers,* and two other books be returned to the library shelves.

The school board disregarded the committee's recommendations, agreeing only to return *Laughing Boy* and *Black Boy* to the library shelves, but the latter only on a restricted basis. School board President Richard Ahrens responded to critics by saying, "It is not only our right but our duty to make the decision, and we would do it again in the face of the abuse heaped upon us by the media."

But the controversy was only beginning. On January 4, 1977, five area students, led by former student council President Steven Pico, filed a suit against the school district. They sought an injunction against the board to have the nine banned books returned to the school libraries. They claimed that the school board had violated their constitutional rights by removing the books. The case went before a federal district court, and in August 1979 the court decided in favor of the school board. The decision, bought down by Judge George C. Pratt, ruled that school boards have the right to determine the "suitability" of library materials.

The students refused to admit defeat. They took the case to the Circuit Court of Appeals and on October 2, 1980, the three-judge panel voted 2 to 1 in favor of the students—reversing the district court's decision. The judges ordered a trial to decide if the students' constitutional rights under the First Amendment had been violated. The U.S. Supreme Court agreed to hear the case, based on the fact that the two lower courts could not agree.

The Supreme Court heard oral arguments from both sides on March 2, 1982. The board's attorney, George W. Lipp, Jr., stressed that the nine books were not just mildly offensive but contained "indecent matter, vulgarities, profanities, descriptions of sexual relations [and] some [insulting] remarks about blacks, Jews, or Christians." He also argued that the students' rights were not being violated, since they could obtain the books at the public library or elsewhere. Alan H. Levine, a lawyer for the NYCLU, countered that "[w]hile schools do transmit values, they may not ignore their obligations to respect diversity."

After considerable deliberation, the Supreme Court handed down its decision on June 25. In a 5 to 4 vote, the Court ruled in favor of the students and ordered the case to be tried back in the district court to get to the bottom of the school board's reasons for the banning. Speaking for the majority, Justice William Brennan declared that "we hold that local school boards may not remove books from school library shelves simply because they dislike the ideas contained in those books." Steven Pico and his fellow students were pleased with the outcome. "It's a clear victory for the First Amendment," Pico said.

Chief Justice William Burger, speaking for the minority opinion, stated that if the plurality's view were "to become the law, this court would come perilously close to becoming a 'super censor' of school board library decisions." He added, "I categorically reject this notion that the Constitution dictates that judges, rather than parents, teachers, and local school boards, must determine how the standards of morality and vulgarity are to be treated in the classroom."

Rather than go through another trial, the Island Trees school board voted 6 to 1 on August 12, 1982, to return the nine books to the school libraries. "Going to trial is like playing Russian roulette, except for us there would be four bullets and one empty chamber," explained board Vice President Frank Martin. Christina Fasulo, the lone dissenter, said, "I cannot in good conscience return filth to a school library when they have access to the book at a public library."

The board did make one requirement concerning the nine books. They would only be loaned to students with a note to parents that read: "The Board of Education wishes to inform you that the book(s) selected by your child may contain materials, which you may find objectionable." Four months later, the New York State Attorney General's Office ordered the board to remove the notes and the red "Parental Notification" stamps from the books, claiming that they violated state law guaranteeing the privacy of library records.

## More Recent Challenges

Book censorship was dealt a major blow in the Island Trees case, but the challenges against *Black Boy* in local school districts continued. In 1994 in Oxford, North Carolina, parents of students objected to the book's "filthy words," "lustful talk," "immoral sex," and "the putting down of ALL kinds of people: the boy's family, the white people, the Jew, the church, the church school, and even his friends."

In 1996 Nelda Click, school board member of the Round Rock Independent School District in Texas, asked for the removal of *Black Boy, Native Son,* and 10 other books from the reading lists of two local high schools. One parent felt Wright's novels should be banned for the simple reason that they were "written while the author was a member of the Communist Party." The board voted down Click's motion 4 to 2. However, members did agree to create a curriculum council to help develop a permanent policy for selecting school reading materials.

In May 1997 the Reverend Dale Shaw, president of the North Florida Ministerial Alliance, launched an attack on *Black Boy,* demanding its removal from Jacksonville, Florida, public schools. "It has historical value," Shaw conceded. "But that doesn't make it right for high school students."

This challenge brought a response from an unexpected quarter, Richard Wright's 84-year-old widow. In a letter to the *Florida Times-Union,* Ellen Wright wrote, "That such a record of survival against inhuman odds should be suppressed after fifty years of being fruitfully taught in our nation's schools would be tantamount to an American tragedy. *Black Boy* tells of a long-ago child who was not allowed to read books. Do we want this book denial to be repeated in today's South?"

## Further Reading

Foerstel, Herbert N. *Banned in the U.S.A.: A Reference Guide to Book Censorship in Schools and Public Libraries.* Westport, Conn.: Greenwood Press, 2002.

Hall, Barbara. "Book Banning is Alive, Complex, and Contested." *Boston Globe,* July 3, 1983: 1.

"Jacksonville, Florida." *Newsletter on Intellectual Freedom,* September 1997: 127.

Karolides, Nicholas J. *Banned Books: Literature Suppressed on Political Grounds.* New York: Facts On File, 2006.

Karolides, Nicholas J., Margaret Bald, and Dawn B. Sova. *120 Banned Books: Censorship Histories of World Literature.* New York: Facts On File, 2005.

"Providence, Rhode Island." *Newsletter on Intellectual Freedom,* March 1971: 35.

Rogers, Donald J. *Banned! Book Censorship in the Schools.* New York: Messner, 1988.

Rowley, Hazel. *Richard Wright: The Life and Times.* New York: Henry Holt, 2001.

"Victory! Island Trees Board Throws in the Towel." *Newsletter on Intellectual Freedom,* November 1982: 197.

## About the Author of *Black Boy*

### Richard Wright (1908–1960)

Richard Wright was the first African-American writer to become a major novelist. His fame today rests on two books that have become American classics—*Native Son* (1940) and the autobiographical *Black Boy* (1945).

Wright was born on September 4, 1908, on a plantation 25 miles north of Natchez, Mississippi. His grandfather was a runaway slave who came North to join the Union Navy immediately after the Civil War. His father was a sharecropper and a mill worker. His mother was a country schoolteacher.

When Richard was four, the family moved to Memphis, Tennessee, where his father abandoned them. During his mother's serious illness, Richard and his younger brother lived in an orphanage. After that, he was shuttled around to a series of relatives, developing a reputation as a tough, unreachable child. About 1920, he and his brother were reunited with their mother and went to live with an aunt and uncle in Oklahoma. One night, Richard's uncle was lynched by a group of white men.

At age 15, Wright had his first story published in a local black newspaper. He left school in the ninth grade and moved to Memphis, where he worked at menial jobs and read voraciously. He later moved to Chicago to pursue writing, but the only job he could get was in the post office, a job he lost in 1929 when the Great Depression began. Disillusioned by the capitalist system, Wright became a Communist and wrote for Communist journals.

In 1937 he moved to New York City and became the editor of the Harlem bureau of the *Daily Worker,* a Communist newspaper. The next year his first book, *Uncle Tom's Children,* a collection of four long stories, was published. *Native Son* (1940), a novel based on the real murder of a white woman by a black youth, brought him fame, fortune, and critical praise. His reputation was confirmed by *Black Boy,* published in 1945. By then, Wright had left the Communist Party, but he was unhappy with the racism he continued to experience despite his celebrity.

In 1946 he accepted an invitation from the French government to visit that country. Overwhelmed by the lack of racism against minorities in France, he decided to stay and never returned permanently to the United States again. Wright's remaining literary output was wildly uneven, and some critics felt that a falling off in his work was due partly to the fact that he had lost touch with America by living in self-imposed exile. Wright attempted to move to England, but was refused a visa and returned to France, where he died on November 28, 1960. According to his will, he was cremated and his ashes mixed with the ashes of a copy of *Black Boy.*

# *Animal Farm* (1945)
## by George Orwell

### What Happens in *Animal Farm*

Set on a fictional farm in England, *Animal Farm* is a political satire that uses animals as its main characters. Old Major, a pig, describes a dream he had to the other animals at Mr. Jones's Manor Farm. In his dream, all animals live free and independent of their human masters, a philosophy he calls Animalism.

Although Old Major dies soon after, the animals are inspired by Animalism and plan a revolt against Farmer Jones. The rebellion is led by two pigs, Snowball and Napoleon. Under their strong leadership, the animals drive Jones and his men off the farm and take it over for themselves, renaming it Animal Farm. The animals agree on Seven Commandments of Animalism, which they will live by and paint on the barn wall. The most important rule is "All animals are equal."

The pigs, who have proven their leadership skills, oversee the farm, but initially everyone has a say in how things are run. Jones later attempts to retake the farm, but is defeated by the animals, under Snowball's skillful leadership, in the Battle of the Cowshed.

During the long winter months, Snowball draws up plans for a windmill to provide electricity for the farm and make all their lives easier. Napoleon, however, is against the building of the windmill. When the animals gather to vote for or against the windmill, Napoleon summons a pack of dogs under his control, and they chase Snowball off the farm.

Napoleon then assumes control of the farm and becomes a dictator. He claims the windmill was his idea, stolen by Snowball, and under his orders it is built. Boxer, a horse, works tirelessly to construct the windmill. One by one, the commandments are broken or revised by Napoleon and the other pigs: Napoleon has dealings with neighboring human farmers, moves into the farmhouse with his cronies, and sleeps in a bed. When Boxer collapses from overwork, the heartless Napoleon sells him to a glue factory while telling the other animals that Boxer died peacefully in a veterinarian's hospital.

Time passes and Animal Farm prospers, but only for the benefit of Napoleon and the other pigs. Just one of the seven commandments has been retained, but with a significant change: "All animals are equal" now concludes with "but some are more equal than others." In the novel's final scene, Napoleon is in the farmhouse entertaining the neighboring human farmers he has dealings with. As the other animals watch them play cards through the window, they cannot tell the pigs apart from the humans.

From the beginning, *Animal Farm* faced numerous challenges—both from the Soviet government and from people who worried about the Soviets' reaction to the book.

## Challenges and Censorship

"I am writing a little squib [satirical work], which might amuse you when it comes out," George Orwell told a friend in February 1943. "But it is not so OK politically that I don't feel certain in advance that anyone will publish."

Orwell's feelings about his latest work, the political fable *Animal Farm*, were accurate. While ostensibly about a group of animals that revolt against their owner and take over their farm, it was really about the 1917 Bolshevik Revolution in Russia and the ruthless rise in the 1920s of dictator Joseph Stalin in what became the Soviet Union.

Orwell, who had previously admired the Bolsheviks (later known as Communists), came to change his opinion of them during the Spanish Civil War of 1936–39. Orwell joined the Republicans, who ran the democratically elected government of Spain, to fight against the rebelling Nationalists, led by military leader Francisco Franco. The Soviets supported the Republicans in the war, but Orwell gradually realized that the Soviets were more interested in exerting their own control over the Republicans than in helping their cause. "Many of our friends were shot, and others spent a long time in prison or simply disappeared," Orwell later wrote.

He recalled how he first got the idea for *Animal Farm* in a preface to a 1947 Ukrainian edition of the novel: "On my return from Spain I thought of exposing the Soviet myth in a story that could be easily understood by almost anyone . . . However, the actual details of the story did not come to me for some time until one day I saw a little boy, perhaps ten years old, driving a huge cart-horse along a narrow path, whipping it whenever it tried to turn. It struck me that if only such animals became aware of their strength we should have no power over them, and that men exploit animals in much the same way as the rich exploit the proletariat [working class]. I proceeded to analyse Marx's [Karl Marx, founder of Communism] theory from the animals' point of view . . . ."

# Landmark Challenge: A Fable That Was All Too Real

When Orwell sent the manuscript of *Animal Farm* to Victor Gollancz, a Soviet sympathizer who had published several of his earlier books, the publisher wrote to Orwell's agent: "I am highly critical of many aspects of internal and external Soviet policy: but I could not possibly publish . . . a general attack of this nature."

Orwell was not surprised by Gollancz's rejection; he had, in fact, anticipated it. He was more surprised when Jonathan Cape, who had initially been enthusiastic about the work, later had second thoughts. These thoughts came after Cape was advised not to publish *Animal Farm* by Peter Smollett, an official in the British government's Ministry of Information. Smollett was later discovered to be a Soviet spy.

"I can see now that it might be regarded as something which it was highly ill-advised to publish at the present time," Cape wrote Orwell. "If the fable were addressed generally to dictators and dictatorships at large then publication would be all right, but the fable does follow, as I feel now, so completely the progress and development of the Russian Soviets and their two dictators [Stalin and Trotsky, represented by Napoleon and Snowball], that it can apply only to Russia, to the exclusion of the dictatorships." Cape went on to suggest that Orwell make the chief villains animals other than pigs. "I think the choice of pigs as the ruling caste will no doubt give offense to many people, and particularly to anyone who is a bit touchy, as usually the Russians are . . . ."

Fortunately Orwell disregarded this advice. The reason Cape and many other Britons were so acutely sensitive to Russian feelings was that Britain was at war against Nazi Germany, and the Soviet Union was one of Britain's principal allies. The breakup of that alliance, and the Soviet takeover of much of Eastern Europe, was still several years away.

Orwell next turned to his friend and fellow writer T. S. Eliot, who was a partner in the publishing firm of Faber and Faber. While Eliot recognized the literary merit of *Animal Farm,* he felt it was not "our kind of book" due to its political nature.

Fred Warburg, of Secker and Warburg, finally agreed to publish *Animal Farm,* but it did not appear until August 1945, the month World War II ended with the surrender of Japan. Orwell was apprehensive that the book would fail, partly because of its short length. At one point he had even considered publishing it himself in pamphlet form.

But *Animal Farm* was successful beyond its author's wildest dreams. The first printing of 4,500 copies sold out in a month. Ten thousand more copies were immediately printed. The reviews were mostly laudatory. Critic Cyril Connolly praised the novel for having "the feeling, the penetration, and the verbal economy of Orwell's master [Jonathan] Swift."

Poet and critic William Empson's praise was more cautious. "I think it worth warning you (while thanking you very heartily) that you must expect to be 'misunderstood' on a large scale about this book," he wrote Orwell in a letter. "It is a form that inherently means more than the author means, when it is handled sufficiently well."

Empson's assessment was an accurate one. Many readers read into *Animal Farm* what they wanted to. Conservative critics took it as an anti-socialist tract, when in fact Orwell remained a devoted socialist until his death. Leftists saw it as an unfair attack on Communism, when the author was really attacking all dictatorships. "I did mean it to have a wider application in so much that I meant that that kind of revolution . . . can only lead to a change of masters," Orwell later wrote. "What I was trying to say was, 'You can't have a revolution unless you make it for yourself; there is no such thing as a benevolent dictat[or]ship."

Orwell had written a special preface entitled "The Freedom of the Press," expressing his thoughts on censorship, but it was dropped from many later editions of the book. Whether Orwell withdrew it voluntarily or if it was itself a victim of censorship is uncertain to this day. "The sinister fact about literary censorship in England is that it is largely voluntary," he wrote in the preface. "[Things are] kept right out of the British press, not because the Government intervened but because of a general tacit agreement that 'it wouldn't do' to mention that particular fact."

## Landmark Challenge: The American View

The novel did not appear in the United States until 1946, after being turned down by a number of publishers. The Dial Press rejected it, saying that "it was impossible to sell animal stories in the U.S.A." Other American publishers thought the book too slight or too critical of the Russians.

Harcourt Brace in New York City finally took a chance on Orwell's fable and was very happy it did. The book was immediately chosen as a Book-of-the-Month Club selection, selling more than half a million copies through that organization alone. By the end of 1946, *Animal Farm* was the second-best-selling book of the year in the United States, outsold only by Dr. Benjamin Spock's *Pocket Book of Baby and Child Care*. By that time there were nine foreign editions of the novel.

The American reviews were wide ranging. Critic Edmund Wilson praised Orwell for working "out his theme with a simplicity, a wit, and a dryness," and compared his writing to Jonathan Swift and French satirist Voltaire. On the other hand, Isaac Rosenfeld in the *Nation* found the book "a disappointing piece of work." Orville Prescott wrote in the *Yale Review*, "As a satire of Russian totalitarianism *Animal Farm* is . . . completely inconclusive . . . He [Orwell] has no suggestions to make as to how such a disaster could be prevented."

Since Orwell's death in 1950, *Animal Farm* has remained extremely popular on high school reading lists. Teachers view it as the kind of straightforward, entertaining allegory that students can understand and appreciate. But it has also remained controversial and has often been challenged.

# Landmark Challenge:
## *Animal Farm* the Play Makes a Quick Exit

In 1986 the International Theatre Institute (ITI), a nongovernmental organization founded by the United Nations Educational, Scientific, and Cultural Organization (UNESCO), held its Theater of Nations Festival in Baltimore, Maryland. It was the first time in its 30-year history that the festival was being held in North America. Among the 13 countries participating was Great Britain, whose National Theatre was to present a stage adaptation of *Animal Farm* under the direction of Sir Peter Hall.

"We thought it was old enough to be a classic, at least a contemporary one," said ITI vice president Martha Coigney. "It was chosen in theatrical innocence, and we were wrong to think that it would not cause problems."

Several months before the festival was to take place, Nigerian playwright Wole Soyinka, president of ITI, received a visit from a Soviet representative who expressed his country's displeasure with the British offering. "I pointed out to them that 'Animal Farm' was a novel that could be applied to many situations," Soyinka said. "They said they had seen it [in London] and presented me with a copy of the program. There is no question that the program was virulent against the Soviet Union. We told them point-blank that the program could be changed. However, they insisted that the play itself was offensive."

Soyinka flew to London, saw the production for himself, and agreed with the representative that it was definitely anti-Soviet. Soyinka, himself once a victim of totalitarianism in his native land, now faced a serious dilemma. The Soviet Union, while it had no production in the festival, was an important member of ITI. Four other Soviet bloc nations—Poland, Czechoslovakia, Hungary, and Bulgaria—all had productions in the festival. If *Animal Farm* was performed as scheduled, the Soviets threatened to have their four satellites withdraw from the festival. Article 1 of the ITI's charter stated, "The organization shall be guided by the principle of mutual respect of the national traditions of each country." Soyinka and other ITI officials did not want to drive five nations, and possibly more, from an organization formed in peace and friendship.

Soyinka appealed to the National Theatre and Hall to work out a settlement in private with the Soviets. They refused. A compromise of sorts was worked out, but not to the liking of the National Theatre. Its production of *Animal Farm* would be performed at the Morris A. Mechanic Theater in Baltimore during the festival but not as a part of it.

"It really isn't censorship if what happens here is that *Animal Farm* will be playing in Baltimore right in the middle of the festival," said festival producer T. Edward Hambleton. "Saying that this isn't censorship is Orwellian double talk," responded Hall. "I think it would make Orwell double up with laughter."

Within days of the announcement, the American theater world responded. "We start wandering into an uncharted sea when we respond to requests to withdraw works of political opinion," said Martin E. Segal, chairman of the board of the Lincoln Center for the Performing Arts in New York City. "Theater to be relevant is in many areas one of the last ramparts of truly free speech and expression," stated actress Colleen Dewhurst, president of Actors Equity at the time. "It's dangerous to give in to censorship by other countries or influences in our own country."

But some people were sympathetic to Soyinka and his decision. "The obvious liberal point of view is the usual feeling that anyone in the arts should be concerned about censorship," responded Joseph Papp, director of New York's Public Theater. "On the other hand, the purpose of the festival is to create harmony among nations . . . In this day and age, you have to work things out together. The festival is important for that reason."

The debate between the two principals—Soyinka and Hall—grew ugly and personal. "Peter Hall is going on an ego trip to suggest that the play has been censored," said Soyinka. " . . . He has given a distorted picture of the whole thing . . . I think it is sheer opportunism to present himself as a knight and defender of civil liberties and we others as philistines [people indifferent to cultural values]."

Hall, who declined an invitation from Soyinka to debate him publicly, agreed that the promotion of international relations was important, "but not at any price." "I do not believe the ITI should have asked me to connive at an act of censorship," Hall said. " . . . I believe in intellectual understanding but only if it is built on honesty."

That June, the festival went on without further incident, as did the production of *Animal Farm*. And within five years, in the face of growing resistance within the Soviet bloc and the reforms of a new leader, Mikhail Gorbachev, the Soviet Union dissolved itself and the

Communist regimes of Eastern Europe crumbled. And somewhere George Orwell, if not laughing, was at least smiling.

In 1995, on the fiftieth anniversary of *Animal Farm*'s publication, the book was again hailed by critics to be as relevant as ever. Communism may have died in the Soviet Union, but many of the world's peoples still lived under dictatorships. "[I]n *Animal Farm*," wrote author Russell Baker in the preface to the fiftieth-anniversary edition, "Orwell left us a lesson about the human contribution to political terror that will always be as up-to-date as next year's elections."

"Some animals are more equal than others. Some classics are more equal than others," wrote one perceptive critic in the *Economist*. He may have been referring to the fact that since its first publication, *Animal Farm* has never gone out of print.

## Further Reading

Bennetts, Leslie. "Soviet Protest Bars Orwell Play from Festival." *New York Times,* May 24, 1986: 1.1.

Bowker, Gordon. *Inside George Orwell.* New York: Palgrave Macmillan, 2003.

Crick, Bernard. *George Orwell: A Life.* Boston: Little, Brown, 1980.

Davison, Peter. *George Orwell: A Literary Life.* New York: St. Martin's Press, 1996.

Karolides, Nicholas J. *Banned Books: Literature Suppressed on Political Grounds.* New York: Facts On File, 2006.

Kleiman, Dena. "Festival's Ban on Orwell Gets Mixed Reaction." *New York Times,* May 29, 1986: C19.

_____. "Storm Over 'Animal Farm' Dispute." *New York Times,* May 31, 1986: 1.11.

## About the Author of *Animal Farm*

### George Orwell (1903–1950)

George Orwell—novelist, essayist, and social critic—was one of the most celebrated English writers of the first half of the twentieth century. He was born Eric Arthur Blair on June 25, 1903, in Motihari, Bengal, India, the son of an English civil servant. He later moved to England with his family and attended Eton, a leading preparatory school, from 1917 to 1921.

In 1922 he moved to Burma, a British colony, to serve in the Indian Imperial Police. Orwell wrote about his experiences of this period in the novel *Burmese Days* (1934) and the classic essay "Shooting an Elephant" (1936). His five years in Burma turned Orwell into an anti-imperialist and a socialist.

He returned to England in 1927 and wandered around the country and Europe, living a vagabond life of poverty. Orwell wrote about these experiences in *Down and Out in Paris and London* (1933). His developing empathy for working-class people was the focus of several novels of this period, including *A Clergyman's Daughter* (1935), *Keep the Aspidistra Flying* (1936), and *Coming Up for Air* (1939).

During the Spanish Civil War he briefly served as a soldier with the Republicans against the fascist Nationalists and suffered a near-fatal throat wound. In his book about this time, *Homage to Catalonia* (1938), Orwell wrote of his disenchantment with the Soviet Communists who allied themselves with the Republicans. Orwell remained a staunch socialist but anti-Communist for the rest of his life.

Despite his prolific output, Orwell did not become a well-known writer until the publication of *Animal Farm* in 1945. His last novel, *1984,* was a shattering depiction of a future totalitarian state. Always in fragile health, Orwell died of tuberculosis in London on January 21, 1950.

# *The Catcher in the Rye* (1951)
## by J. D. Salinger

• • • • • • • • • • • • •

## What Happens in *The Catcher in the Rye*

*The Catcher in the Rye* is the story of Holden Caulfield, a confused 16-year-old boy, who narrates the novel. The entire book's action takes place over the two days that Holden leaves the private boarding school where he is failing and returns unannounced to New York City, his home. During much of the novel Holden wanders around the city, having encounters, both humorous and sad, with a number of people, including an old schoolmate he detests, a former girlfriend, a prostitute, and a former teacher, who may or may not have made sexual advances toward him.

Although he exerts a tough exterior and smokes, drinks, and swears, Holden is a sensitive young man in search of a purpose in life amid the "phoniness" of adult society. In the novel's finale, he meets with his beloved sister, 10-year-old Phoebe, whom he longs to protect from the world. He tells her of his ambition to be the "catcher in the rye"—a person who watches over children playing in a field of high grass and catches them before they tumble over a hidden cliff.

Salinger's supposedly plotless novel is a concise and touching portrait of an adolescent in crisis, possibly the best coming-of-age novel produced by an American author. It remains a popular and much-admired literary classic and was ranked sixty-fourth on the Modern Library's list of the 100 best English-language novels of the twentieth century.

## Challenges and Censorship

When first published in 1951, *The Catcher in the Rye* was like a splash of ice water in the placid face of American postwar society. No American writer had depicted the anger, confusion, and sensibility of adolescence so clearly or so honestly since Mark Twain in *The Adventures of Huckleberry Finn*.

But Huck was a child of the American past, while 16-year-old Holden Caulfield was a contemporary youth in a modern world. It's little wonder that, like Twain's novel, *The Catcher in the Rye* has been both cherished as a classic and denounced as an attack on American values. It ranks thirteenth in the American Library Association's "100 Most Frequently Challenged Books of 1990–2000." The People for the American Way ranked it second on its list of most frequently challenged books from 1982 to 1996.

Attempts to censor or ban Salinger's book began in the mid-1950s and grew in number through the 1960s and 1970s. The reactions of parents and others were generally more vehement than in challenges to other books, perhaps because Holden, the narrator and protagonist, questions and criticizes everything in adult society.

## Landmark Challenge: The Runaway Advisory Board

When David Schmidt, chairman of the Shawnee Mission South School District's Advisory Board in Kansas, left the board meeting on January 17, 1972, he thought all new business was finished. He later found out he was very wrong.

The remaining members listened to fellow member Florence DuBois read a letter from a "patron" who objected to *The Catcher in the Rye* and urged its removal from the local high school's supplemental reading list. Immediately after, the board members voted unanimously to recommend the book's removal to the district school board.

Chairman Schmidt was stunned when he heard the news and branded his colleagues "vigilantes and witch-hunters" as well as "self-appointed censors." His outrage was supported by many people in the community. The number of phone calls to the district's newsline doubled the day after the report of the action. Of the 200 calls received, none supported the advisory board's action.

"At no time was the word 'ban' used and we did not suggest removal of the book from the libraries," said board member Marilyn Mayberry, in the group's defense. "A proposal, never moved or voted upon, was made to form a committee to study district materials and make recommendations. The vitriolic reaction to erroneous reporting on the meeting has been overwhelming."

Some parents of South High School students were more open and frank in their dislike for the novel. Mrs. Clifford R. Putzier called Salinger "an early supporter of sin." "After his divorce," she continued, "he became more and more withdrawn from society, proving he had not learned the lesson set down in his own book . . . If these opinions make me a witch-hunter, a vigilante, then so be it."

On the other side of the issue, a representative of the organization People Dedicated to Quality (PDQ) acknowledged that advisory boards "provide a valuable function," but declared that "the professional staff, by virtue of their specialized training and their professional integrity, is qualified to determine what should be included in the curriculum and when and how it should be taught."

At the next advisory board meeting, on February 1, Schmidt allowed each board member to speak his or her mind before another vote was taken on *The Catcher in the Rye*. This time, the board voted against the banning of the novel.

The *Kansas City Star*, which covered the incident, summed up its feelings in an editorial: "People who want to impose their personal beliefs on an entire community or tell others what they cannot read ought to be regarded with some caution. They mean well, they work very hard, and they can do a lot of damage."

# Landmark Challenge: Big Doings in a Small Town

Boron, population about 4,000, is a quiet little town near the Mojave Desert in Southern California. That quiet was disrupted in September 1989, when a book challenge rocked the town.

It all started when Vickie Swindler learned that her 14-year-old daughter, Brook, had been assigned *The Catcher in the Rye* in her English class at Boron High School. Objecting to the book's foul language, Swindler found herself using some strong language herself. "I called the school," she later recalled, "and I said, 'How the hell did this teacher get this book?'" She then launched a personal crusade to get the book off the state-approved supplemental reading list, calling her friends and reading them passages from the novel. With the support of friends and fellow parents, Swindler convinced the school board to remove the book from the reading list by a vote of 4 to 1.

"There's 69 other books on that list," said board head Jim Sommers. "I'm sure they'll find another good one. The students are going to get a full and complete education without that book."

"Yes, there's harshness and profanity in society," admitted F. O. Roe, another board member. "But we don't have to accept them, just the same as we don't have to accept the narcotics that are in the streets and the murders that are happening all over the country."

For English teacher Shelley Keller-Gage, one of the teachers who assigned *The Catcher in the Rye* to her students, the problem was not the world that the book reflected as much as the good people of Boron themselves. "These people are being just like Holden [Caulfield, the protagonist], the ones who are trying to censor the book. They are trying to be catchers in the rye. They're wanting to preserve the innocence of the children, and I think that instead of trying to preserve their innocence, we have to try to deal with these children losing their innocence. I think society is the one that is kind of taking the innocence away. Things are not innocent anymore, and I think we've got to help them deal with that, to make reasonable choices, to be responsible citizens."

The alternative book Keller-Gage offered her students in lieu of Salinger's novel was a telling choice. It was Ray Bradbury's *Fahrenheit 451,* a science-fiction novel that deals with the subject of book burning.

As for *Catcher in the Rye,* it was enjoying a new popularity at the Boron public library. The librarian reported a waiting list of 15 people who wanted to read this high-school-banned book.

## Landmark Challenge: Challenging the Challenge

A challenge in North Berwick, Maine, against *The Catcher in the Rye* led to a constructive rethinking of public school policy dealing with challenges. When their 14-year-old son brought the book home from Noble High School in the fall of 2005, Andrea and Mike Minnon of Lebanon, Maine, were appalled by the language and antisocial behavior of Holden Caulfield. The Minnons called for the book to be banned from the school's curriculum.

The school board took the challenge seriously and formed an 11-member Educational Materials Review Committee made up of administrators, teachers, parents, students, school board members, and the school's head librarian. On December 15, 2005, meeting in closed session, the committee listened to testimony from English teachers who valued the book as a teaching tool. They claimed it helped students deal with their fears and their place in society. Two days later the committee issued the unanimous opinion that *Catcher in the Rye* be retained in ninth grade, "based on the themes and essential questions within the curriculum, which was shared by the representatives at the meeting."

The Minnons were not surprised by the decision, but voiced their disappointment. "It's socially unacceptable to use all those [curse] words in the work environment, and they claim the schools are their work environment, yet they're promoting a book that has all these swears in it," said Andrea Minnon. "I'm disgusted and ashamed that a school that claims it has such high standards and wants to look a certain way is using materials like this."

But while upholding the novel's use, the committee made a series of recommendations for all future challenges. It called for teachers to provide parents with a rationale about the books they taught and how the material fit in with the curriculum. It also asked for the creation of a "teacher-parent resource binder" that would hold reviews of the books and other teaching materials. The committee recommended a review of the existing Citizen's Challenge to Educational Review form, to allow parents to better express their concerns about the materials they are challenging. Finally, the committee recommended a list of alternative books that would be made available to parents who preferred their children not read this book.

But Andrea Minnon would not retreat from her position. "He [her son] is definitely not reading it," she said. "I don't want my kids learning the trash that they're promoting." Trash or treasure, *Catcher in the Rye* will continue to challenge readers for many years to come.

# Further Reading

"'Catcher' Catches It . . . Again." *Newsletter on Intellectual Freedom,* May 1972: 88.

Foerstel, Herbert N. *Banned in the U.S.A.: A Reference Guide to Book Censorship in Schools and Public Libraries.* Westport, Conn.: Greenwood Press, 2002.

Green, Jonathon, and Nicholas J. Karolides. *Encyclopedia of Censorship, New Edition.* New York: Facts On File, 2005.

Mydans, Seth. "In a Small Town, a Battle Over a Book." *New York Times,* September 3, 1989: 22.

"North Berwick, Maine." *Newsletter on Intellectual Freedom,* March 2005: 73–74. Available online: https://members.ala.org/nif/v54n2/success_stories.html.

Sova, Dawn B. *Banned Books: Literature Suppressed on Social Grounds.* New York: Facts On File, 2006.

# About the Author of *The Catcher in the Rye*

## J. D. Salinger (1919–   )

No American author has written so little and yet been as heralded, analyzed, and written about as J. D. Salinger. Jerome David Salinger was born on January 1, 1919, in New York City. His father was a Polish Jew who worked for a meat importer. His mother was of Scots-Irish descent. Salinger graduated from Valley Forge Military Academy in 1936 and attended several colleges over the next few years, but never earned a degree. He found a mentor in Whit Burnett, editor of *Story* magazine, whose creative-writing class he took at Columbia University. Burnett published Salinger's first story, "The Young Folks," in 1940.

Salinger was drafted into the Army in 1942 and served as a staff sergeant in World War II, seeing heavy action at Utah Beach during the D-Day invasion and at the Battle of the Bulge. He was later one of the first American soldiers to enter a liberated concentration camp. The experience left him hospitalized for several weeks with combat stress reaction.

After the war, Salinger's stories appeared in a number of magazines, including *Collier's,* the *Saturday Evening Post,* and the *New Yorker.* In 1948 his story "A Perfect Day for Bananafish" appeared in the *New Yorker* and was highly praised. After that, Salinger signed a special contract with the *New Yorker* and nearly all his subsequent stories appeared exclusively in that magazine.

In 1951, at age 31, Salinger published his only novel and most celebrated book, *The Catcher in the Rye*. By 2004, it had sold more than ten million copies. Salinger was uncomfortable with the great celebrity that came with his fame, and in 1953 he moved from New York City to the remote village of Cornish, New Hampshire, where he still lives today.

His *Nine Stories* (1955) was well received and began the saga of the Glass family. Two more volumes followed, containing two novellas each: *Franny and Zooey* (1961) and *Raise High the Roof Beam, Carpenters* (1963). In 1965 the *New Yorker* published his novella "Hapworth 16, 1924"—his last published work to date. In a rare 1970s interview the writer claimed to write daily and find great pleasure in it, but viewed publication as "a terrible invasion of his privacy."

In 1997, it was announced that a small publisher would put out "Hapworth 16, 1924" in book form, but Salinger later changed his mind. He remains a legendary, reclusive figure in American literature. He has been married to his third wife, Colleen O'Neill, a nurse and quiltmaker, since 1988.

# *To Kill a Mockingbird* (1960)
## by Harper Lee

### What Happens in *To Kill a Mockingbird*

*To Kill a Mockingbird* is the story of a race trial in a small Alabama town during the 1930s. A black man, Tom Robinson, is accused of raping a white woman, Mayella Ewell, and is defended by Atticus Finch, a morally upstanding country lawyer. The events, covering a period of three years, are narrated by Jean Louise Finch, better known as Scout, Atticus's daughter, looking back at the period as she experienced it as a child. A major subplot is Scout's efforts, with her older brother Jem and summer visitor Dill, to lure their mysterious and reclusive neighbor Arthur "Boo" Radley from his house.

During Robinson's trial, Atticus proves beyond a doubt that the black man, with his withered left arm, could not have made the bruises on the right side of Mayella's face. It becomes clear, as the trial progresses, that it was Mayella who tried to seduce an unwilling Tom. When her brutal father, Bob Ewell, discovered them together, he beat Mayella and then coerced her to blame it on Robinson.

Despite the weight of the evidence, the all-white jury, prejudiced against Tom and unwilling to admit that he is better than the Ewells, convict him. Later Tom is killed while trying to escape prison, putting an end to Atticus's attempts for an appeal. But Bob Ewell, exposed by Atticus, still thirsts for revenge. When he attempts to stab Jem and Scout with his knife, Boo Radley finally emerges from his house and rescues them, killing Ewell.

# Challenges and Censorship

*To Kill a Mockingbird* has been hailed as one of the most influential novels in American literature since its publication in 1960. Its message of tolerance and courage in the face of ignorance and racism has been universally embraced by people the world over and has made it one of the most frequently read novels in American secondary schools.

Ironically, Harper Lee's novel has been challenged time and again in schools as racist. According to the American Library Association, it was among the 10 most frequently challenged books in the United States in 1998. It ranked forty-first on the ALA's "100 Most Frequently Challenged Books of 1990–2000."

Why this discrepancy? Like Mark Twain, John Steinbeck, and other American authors before her, Lee remained faithful to the time and place in which her story is set—rural Alabama in the 1930s. "Nigger" was the way many white Southerners referred to a black person in that prejudiced environment, although the protagonist of the book, Atticus Finch, never does. Other words spoken by characters have also been singled out as vulgar or racist.

# Early Challenges

In 1977 the school district of Eden Valley, Minnesota, banned the book temporarily because it contained the words "damn" and "whore lady." The frequent use of the "n" word brought challenges in Warren Township, Indiana, in 1981; Waukegan, Illinois, in 1984; and Park Hill, Mississippi, in 1985. Black parents in the Indiana case also objected to what they called the submissive behavior of such black characters as Tom Robinson, who is accused of raping a white woman, and Calpurnia, the black women who cares for Atticus's children, Scout and Jem. When the Warren Township school board rejected their request to remove the book from schools, three African Americans on the town's human relations advisory committee resigned in protest.

With the support of the National Association for the Advancement of Colored People (NAACP), black parents in Casa Grande East School District in Arizona convinced school officials to move the book from a required junior high school reading list to a supplemental reading list.

In July 1996 in Texas, the Lindale Independent School District board voted unanimously to ban Lee's novel along with thirty-one other books from the Advanced Placement (AP) English reading list because they went against the values of the community. Among the other banned titles were Herman Melville's *Moby-Dick* and Nathaniel Hawthorne's *The Scarlet Letter*. "You have to remember we're in the heart of the Bible Belt," explained high school Principal Jim Bernard, "and this is a very conservative community that is supportive of the school system and our district has to answer to them and listen to their concerns."

## Landmark Challenge: The Censorship Shirt

During the 2003–04 school year, one black eighth-grade student at Stanford Middle School in Durham, North Carolina, found a unique way to voice his protest against the racial slurs in *To Kill a Mockingbird*. Garvey Jackson felt trapped and angry when students in his English class took turns reading passages from the novel. "Just to put it simple, I felt uncomfortable," he said. "Definitely within the first week [of reading it]."

When he told his family about the book and the bad words in it, they were shocked. "We just don't want it in the school system," said his father, Andrew Jackson. "We do want to kill a mockingbird if it takes to the end of the school year."

Garvey, with the full support of his family, decided to dramatize the issue during Black History Month in February 2004. His sister made him a white shirt emblazoned with words and phrases taken from the book. They included "nigger raper," "nigger lover," and "nigger snowman."

Jackson wore the shirt to school but kept it covered. He uncovered it in his English class and strolled to the front of the room, where teacher Thomas Watson stood.

"Basically he said, I should cover that up," recalled Jackson. "I said I wouldn't do that. If it's good enough for the book, it's good enough for the shirt."

Watson sent Jackson to the principal's office, where he was told that the shirt was inappropriate and that he had to replace it with another shirt. No sooner had he taken off the shirt than Jackson's parents arrived at the school to see the effects of his protest. Principal

Dave Ebert explained to the Jacksons that there was a set procedure for challenging books and that Garvey's shirt was against the school's dress code and had to be replaced.

"He was doing the right thing," said his mother, Rita Gonzalez-Jackson. "I agree with him. I support him."

But Garvey Jackson wasn't finished yet. The following week he brought in copies of a letter explaining why the novel was offensive and what should be done about it. He handed them out to his class-mates. Two days later, Watson showed the 1962 film version of *To Kill a Mockingbird*, and Jackson pulled out armbands to pass out to classmates to show their displeasure, but most wouldn't wear them. "They said they made them look ugly," Jackson said.

In a final dramatic gesture, the Jackson family planned a mock funeral for the novel, inviting the entire community to watch as they buried the book in a local cemetery. Garvey's father, Andrew Jackson, called it "Just another form of protest—nonviolent protest. It's not when the book is over, the problem is over."

## Landmark Challenge: Another "Finch" Takes a Stand in Pasadena

Beginning in November 2005, African-American parents and civil rights advocates put pressure on John Finch, head of the private Chandler School in Pasadena, California, to remove Harper Lee's novel from the school's English curriculum.

A committee of African-American families was formed to study the issue. The committee suggested mention of the word "nigger" be left out of any classroom discussions of the book. To further sensitize students to the "n" word, which appears more than 300 times in the novel, Finch had an African-American poet speak to students about the power words hold over people. He also informed students and their parents that any student who used the word outside of class discussion would receive detention or even be suspended.

Jim Morris, whose son is an eighth-grader at the school, was not appeased by these measures. "This letter should not be construed as an attempt at censorship," Morris wrote to other parents. "Rather, it is simply an instance whereby the teaching of a novel, despite its journalistic excellence, will serve to do more harm than good. There is no doubt in my mind that any text which contains an excess of 300 racial slurs . . . would be objected to in any context that was specific to the education of young children."

Morris had the solid support of the Pasadena Branch of the National Association for the Advancement of Colored People (NAACP). "We are trying to get our youngsters to stop using such insensitive words," said NAACP branch President Joe Brown. "If [children] learn those words by age 13, it won't be long before that is imbedded in them. Not the word, but the use of the word . . . It is outrageous that something like this could happen under the guise of education in 2006. What insensitivity."

Some African-American parents did not share Morris's and Brown's concerns. "Our kids are now being exposed to things so much earlier than they used to be," said Nancy McSween, whose eighth-grade daughter, Ariel, enjoyed reading the novel. "If I thought *To Kill a Mockingbird* would hurt my child or cripple my child, I would be picketing."

Ariel herself found the controversy trivial. "In the seventh grade we read a book that had parts about masturbation," she said. "Now we have one that has the 'n' word. And now there is a big controversy?"

School head Finch refused to remove the book from the classroom. "We want to make sure children learn about justice and injustice, and one way to show that is to show negative and positive examples," he said. "*To Kill a Mockingbird* is an important book."

While the controversy and the challenges will continue, the stature of Harper Lee's novel has not been diminished. In a 1991 "Survey of Lifetime Reading Habits" conducted by the Library of Congress's Committee for the Book and the Book-of-the-Month Club, *To Kill a Mockingbird* came in second after the Bible as "making a difference in people's lives."

"*To Kill a Mockingbird* . . . is one of the most moving and effective denunciations of racism ever written," said a 2001 editorial in the *Boston Globe*. "The book teaches tolerance as thoroughly as any modern-day diversity awareness program." In 2007, *To Kill a Mockingbird* was chosen as one of about a dozen books for the nationwide Big Read, a National Endowment for the Arts (NEA) initiative to encourage Americans to read more.

# Further Reading

"Blacklisted in Oklahoma." *Boston Globe*, August 20, 2001, p. A10.

"Durham, North Carolina." *Newsletter on Intellectual Freedom*, May 2004: 98–99. Available online: https://members.ala.org/nif/v53n3/dateline.html.

Foerstel, Herbert N. *Banned in the U.S.A.: A Reference Guide to Book Censorship in Schools and Public Libraries.* Westport, Conn.: Greenwood Press, 2002.

Greene, Jonathon, and Nicholas J. Karolides. *Encyclopedia of Censorship, New Edition.* New York: Facts On File, 2005.

Sova, Dawn B. *Banned Books: Literature Suppressed on Social Grounds.* New York: Facts On File, 2006.

Uhrich, Kevin. "Killing Mockingbirds." *Pasadena Weekly*, March 16, 2006. Available online: www.pasadenaweekly.com/cms/story/detail/killing_mockingbirds/3204. Accessed July 2, 2007.

# About the Author of *To Kill a Mockingbird*

## Harper Lee (1926–   )

Harper Lee has published only one novel to date, but it has earned her a special place in American literature. Nelle Harper Lee was born on April 28, 1926, in the small town of Monroeville, Alabama, the youngest of four children. Her father was a lawyer and a state legislator for 12 years, and is the model for Atticus Finch in *To Kill a Mockingbird*. Like her narrator, Scout, Lee was a tomboy with a lively imagination and a love for reading. Her childhood friend was Truman Capote, who would also become a famous writer and who served as the model for Dill in her novel.

Following in her father's footsteps, Lee entered the University of Alabama in 1945 to study law. While serving as the editor of the campus humor magazine, she began to gravitate toward a writing career. She moved to New York City in 1950 and supported herself as an airline reservationist.

With the financial help of friends, she took off a year from work to write the novel that would eventually become *To Kill a Mockingbird*. She finished the first draft in 1957 and worked nearly three more years on it before it was finally published in 1960. The book was an immediate best seller and earned Lee the Pulitzer Prize in

1961. A movie adaptation followed in 1962, for which Gregory Peck won the Academy Award for Best Actor for his portrayal of Atticus Finch.

The fame that the modest writer experienced during this time was overwhelming. "I hoped for a little [fame] . . . but I got rather a whole lot," she said in a 1964 interview, "and in some ways this was just about as frightening as the quick, merciful death I'd expected."

While rumors of other works in progress have emerged over the years, Lee has published nothing further, aside from a few short essays. She lives quietly and privately, dividing her time between New York City and Monroeville, Alabama. She grants few interviews and rarely gives talks or speeches. Her book continues to be one of the most read and praised of American novels. In 1999 in a *Library Journal* poll, it was voted the "Best Novel of the Century." There are more than 15 million copies of *To Kill a Mockingbird* in print to date.

# APPENDIX 1

# *The American Library Association's "100 Most Frequently Challenged Books of 1990–2000"*

(Books and authors in **boldface** are included in the **Our Freedom to Read** series.)

1. *Scary Stories* **series, by Alvin Schwartz**
2. *Daddy's Roommate,* by Michael Willhoite
3. *I Know Why the Caged Bird Sings,* by Maya Angelou
4. *The Chocolate War,* **by Robert Cormier**
5. *The Adventures of Huckleberry Finn,* **by Mark Twain**
6. *Of Mice and Men,* **by John Steinbeck**
7. *Harry Potter* **series, by J. K. Rowling**
8. *Forever,* **by Judy Blume**
9. *Bridge to Terabithia,* by Katherine Paterson
10. *Alice* **series, by Phyllis Reynolds Naylor**
11. *Heather Has Two Mommies,* by Leslea Newman
12. *My Brother Sam Is Dead,* **by James Lincoln Collier and Christopher Collier**
13. *The Catcher in the Rye,* **by J. D. Salinger**
14. *The Giver,* **by Lois Lowry**
15. *It's Perfectly Normal,* by Robie Harris
16. *Goosebumps* **series**, by R. L. Stine
17. *A Day No Pigs Would Die*, by Robert Newton Peck
18. *The Color Purple,* by Alice Walker
19. *Sex,* by Madonna
20. *Earth's Children* series, by Jean M. Auel

21. *The Great Gilly Hopkins,* **by Katherine Paterson**
22. *A Wrinkle in Time,* **by Madeleine L'Engle**
23. *Go Ask Alice,* **by Anonymous**
24. *Fallen Angels,* **by Walter Dean Myers**
25. *In the Night Kitchen,* **by Maurice Sendak**
26. *The Stupids* series, **by Harry Allard**
27. *The Witches,* **by Roald Dahl**
28. *The New Joy of Gay Sex,* by Charles Silverstein
29. *Anastasia Krupnik* series, by Lois Lowry
30. *The Goats,* **by Brock Cole**
31. *Kaffir Boy,* by Mark Mathabane
32. *Blubber,* **by Judy Blume**
33. *Killing Mr. Griffin,* **by Lois Duncan**
34. *Halloween ABC,* **by Eve Merriam**
35. *We All Fall Down,* **by Robert Cormier**
36. *Final Exit,* by Derek Humphry
37. *The Handmaid's Tale,* by Margaret Atwood
38. *Julie of the Wolves,* **by Jean Craighead George**
39. *The Bluest Eye,* **by Toni Morrison**
40. *What's Happening to My Body? Book for Girls,* by Lynda Madaras
41. *To Kill a Mockingbird,* **by Harper Lee**
42. *Beloved,* by Toni Morrison
43. *The Outsiders,* **by S. E. Hinton**
44. *The Pigman,* **by Paul Zindel**
45. *Bumps in the Night,* by Harry Allard
46. *Deenie,* **by Judy Blume**
47. *Flowers for Algernon,* by Daniel Keyes
48. *Annie on My Mind,* **by Nancy Garden**
49. *The Boy Who Lost His Face,* by Louis Sachar
50. *Cross Your Fingers, Spit in Your Hat,* by Alvin Schwartz
51. *A Light in the Attic,* **by Shel Silverstein**
52. *Brave New World,* **by Aldous Huxley**
53. *Sleeping Beauty Trilogy,* by A. N. Roquelaure (Anne Rice)
54. *Asking About Sex and Growing Up,* by Joanna Cole
55. *Cujo,* **by Stephen King**
56. *James and the Giant Peach,* **by Roald Dahl**
57. *The Anarchist Cookbook,* by William Powell
58. *Boys and Sex,* by Wardell Pomeroy

59. *Ordinary People,* by Judith Guest

60. *American Psycho,* by Bret Easton Ellis

61. *What's Happening to My Body? Book for Boys,* by Lynda Madaras

62. *Are You There God? It's Me, Margaret,* by Judy Blume

63. *Crazy Lady,* by Jane Conly

64. **Athletic Shorts, by Chris Crutcher**

65. *Fade,* by Robert Cormier

66. *Guess What?,* by Mem Fox

67. *The House of Spirits,* by Isabel Allende

68. *The Face on the Milk Carton,* by Caroline Cooney

69. *Slaughterhouse-Five,* by Kurt Vonnegut

70. *Lord of the Flies,* by William Golding

71. *Native Son,* by Richard Wright

72. *Women on Top: How Real Life Has Changed Women's Sexual Fantasies,* by Nancy Friday

73. **Curses, Hexes & Spells, by Daniel Cohen**

74. **Jack, by A.M. Homes**

75. *Bless Me, Ultima,* by Rudolfo A. Anaya

76. *Where Did I Come From?,* by Peter Mayle

77. *Carrie,* by Stephen King

78. *Tiger Eyes,* by Judy Blume

79. *On My Honor,* by Marion Dane Bauer

80. *Arizona Kid,* by Ron Koertge

81. *Family Secrets,* by Norma Klein

82. *Mommy Laid an Egg,* by Babette Cole

83. *The Dead Zone,* by Stephen King

84. **The Adventures of Tom Sawyer, by Mark Twain**

85. *Song of Solomon,* by Toni Morrison

86. *Always Running,* by Luis Rodriguez

87. *Private Parts,* by Howard Stern

88. *Where's Waldo?,* by Martin Hanford

89. **Summer of My German Soldier, by Bette Greene**

90. **Little Black Sambo, by Helen Bannerman**

91. *Pillars of the Earth,* by Ken Follett

92. *Running Loose,* by Chris Crutcher

93. *Sex Education,* by Jenny Davis

94. **The Drowning of Stephan Jones, by Bette Greene**

95. *Girls and Sex,* by Wardell Pomeroy

# APPENDIX 2

## *The American Library Association's "10 Most Frequently Challenged Books of 2006" and the Reasons for the Challenges*

(Books and authors in **boldface** are included in the **Our Freedom to Read** series.)

1. *And Tango Makes Three*, by Justin Richardson and Peter Parnell, for homosexuality, anti-family content, and being unsuited to age group
2. *Gossip Girls* series, by Cecily Von Ziegesar, for homosexuality, sexual content, drugs, being unsuited to age group, and offensive language
3. **Alice series, by Phyllis Reynolds Naylor,** for sexual content and offensive language
4. **The Earth, My Butt, and Other Big Round Things, by Carolyn Mackler,** for sexual content, antifamily content, offensive language, and being unsuited to age group
5. **The Bluest Eye, by Toni Morrison,** for sexual content, offensive language, and being unsuited to age group
6. **Scary Stories series, by Alvin Schwartz,** for occultism/Satanism, being unsuited to age group, violence, and insensitivity
7. **Athletic Shorts, by Chris Crutcher,** for homosexuality and offensive language
8. **The Perks of Being a Wallflower, by Stephen Chbosky,** for homosexuality, sexual content, offensive language, and being unsuited to age group

9. *Beloved,* by Toni Morrison, for offensive language, sexual content, and being unsuited to age group

10. ***The Chocolate War,* by Robert Cormier,** for sexual content, offensive language, and violence

# APPENDIX 3

# The American Library Association's "10 Most Frequently Challenged Books of 2007" and the Reasons for the Challenges

(Books and authors in **boldface** are included in the **Our Freedom to Read** series.)

1. *And Tango Makes Three,* by Justin Richardson and Peter Parnell, for anti-ethnic content, sexism, homosexuality, antifamily content, its religious viewpoint, and being unsuited to age group
2. **The Chocolate War, by Robert Cormier,** for sexual content, offensive language, and violence
3. *Olive's Ocean,* by Kevin Henkes, for sexual content and offensive language
4. **The Golden Compass, by Philip Pullman,** for its religious viewpoint
5. **The Adventures of Huckleberry Finn, by Mark Twain,** for racism
6. *The Color Purple,* by Alice Walker, for homosexuality, sexual content, offensive language, and being unsuited to age group
7. *TTYL,* by Lauren Myracle, for sexual content, offensive language, and being unsuited to age group
8. *I Know Why the Caged Bird Sings,* by Maya Angelou, for sexual content
9. *It's Perfectly Normal,* by Robie Harris, for sexual content
10. **The Perks of Being a Wallflower, by Stephen Chbosky,** for homosexuality, sexual content, offensive language, and being unsuited to age group

# APPENDIX 4

# *Web Sites on Book Censorship and Challenges*

**American Booksellers Foundation for Free Expression**
**www.abffe.org**
*This site is useful for its Banned Books Week Handbook, which includes many interesting features such as "Stories Behind the Bans and Challenges."*

**American Library Association**
**www.ala.org**
*The official Web site of the ALA has a wealth of information on challenged and banned books, including yearly lists of the top challenged books and archives for the ALA's Newsletter on Intellectual Freedom.*

**National Coalition Against Censorship**
**www.ncac.org**
*This site includes updated news on censorship issues, including Supreme Court decisions. There is information on censorship of not only books, but also art, music, science, and entertainment.*

# APPENDIX 5

# *Banned Books Week*

Early each fall, the American Library Association (ALA) sponsors Banned Books Week nationwide. It is an opportunity for everyone who loves to read—and cherishes the freedom to do so—to draw attention to that precious right. The first Banned Books Week was celebrated in 1981.

Here are some ways the ALA's Office for Intellectual Freedom suggests you can celebrate Banned Books Week:

1. Read a banned book. Look for a favorite or something you've never read before on the book lists in appendixes 1, 2, and 3. You might choose one of the books discussed in this volume.
2. Talk about the First Amendment in school. Make it the focus of a class discussion. The First Amendment to the U.S. Constitution reads, "Congress shall make no law respecting an establishment of religion, or prohibiting the free exercise thereof; or abridging the freedom of speech, or of the press; or of the people peaceably to assemble, and to petition the Government for a redress of grievances."
3. Organize your own Banned Books Read-Out! at your school, public library, or local bookstore. Invite a local author, banned or otherwise, to read from his or her work. Have adults and children read selections from banned books.
4. Join IFAN, the Intellectual Freedom Action Network, a grassroots group of volunteers who are willing to come forward in defense of the freedom to read in censorship controversies in your school or community.

5. Join another organization that advocates intellectual freedom, such as the Freedom to Read Foundation.
6. Write or call your government representatives in Washington, D.C., and let them know you want them to protect your freedom to read.

If you have your own ideas for how to celebrate Banned Books Week, e-mail them to the Office for Intellectual Freedom at oif@ala.org. They'd be happy to hear from you!

# Index